LET'S TALK ABOUT IT

SHARING VALUES WITH YOUR KIDS

Allan Hart Jahsmann

BRINGING TRUTH TO LIFE
NavPress Publishing Group
P.O. Box 35001, Colorado Springs, Colorado 80935

The Navigators is an international Christian organization. Our mission is to reach, disciple, and equip people to know Christ and to make Him known through successive generations. We envision multitudes of diverse people in the United States and every other nation who have a passionate love for Christ, live a lifestyle of sharing Christ's love, and multiply spiritual laborers among those without Christ.

NavPress is the publishing ministry of The Navigators. NavPress publications help believers learn biblical truth and apply what they learn to their lives and ministries. Our mission is to stimulate spiritual formation among our readers.

Library of Congress Catalog Card Number: 98-9250
ISBN 1-57683-059-4

Photo by R.W. Jones/Westlight

Some of the anecdotal illustrations in this book are true to life and are included with the permission of the persons involved. All other illustrations are composites of real situations, and any resemblance to people living or dead is coincidental.

Unless otherwise identified, all Scripture quotations in this publication are taken from the New Revised Standard Version (NRSV), copyright 1989, by the Division of Christian Education of the National Council of the Churches of Christ in the USA, used by permission, all rights reserved; the Good News Bible: Today's English Version (TEV), copyright © American Bible Society 1966, 1971, 1976; and the Biblical passages marked The Holy Bible for Children (HBC) edited by Allan Hart Jahsmann, copyrighted 1977 by Concordia Publishing House and used by permission.

Jahsmann, Allan Hart.
     Let's talk about it : sharing values with your kids / Allan Hart Jahsmann.
         p.   cm.
     Includes indexes.
     ISBN 1-57683-059-4 (hardcover)
     1. Christian education—Home training.   2. Christian education of children.
   3. Values—Study and teaching.   I. Title.
BV1590.J34   1998
248.8'45—dc21   98-9250
                                                                     CIP

Printed in the United States of America

1 2 3 4 5 6 7 8 9 10 11 12 13 14 15 / 02 01 00 99 98

CONTENTS

Let's Talk About You

Are You a Bossy Person?   11
What If You Couldn't Remember Anything? 12
What's Your Name? 13
Knowing the Right Time 15
What Do You Want to Be? 16
Remembering What You Promised 18
Your Bag of Gifts 21
The Best Use of Your Time 22
How Good Are Your Manners? 23
Are You Ever Ashamed? 24
What Scares You? 26
Does Your Mother Work? 28
Why Not Admit It? 30
Your Worries and Fears 31
Wishing 33
How Bright a Light Are You? 34
Will You Forgive Me? 36
You Can Be a Peacemaker 37
Avoiding Dangers 39
The Best Way to Be Rich 41

Why Go To School? 42
You and Your Parents 44
Learning Not to Grumble 45
Bad Words and Good Words 46
How Brave Are You? 47
Good Reasons for Reading 50
A Happy Home 51
Things You're Ready to Do 52
Getting an Allowance 54
Deciding Which Way to Go 55
Taking Care of Your Pet 56
What Do You Own? 58
If You Couldn't Hear 59
It's Fun to Work 62
A Good Heart 63
Being a Good Sport 64
Who Are Your Heroes? 65
Let's See Your Teeth 67

Let's Talk About God's World

When It Snows 71
Whatever God Has Made 72
Learning From Geese 73
Wonders in the World 75
The Gifts of Food and Water 77
Bird Nests and Little Birds 78
Going to Faraway Places 79
When It Rains 81

Let's Talk About Jesus and God

How to Say "Thanks" 85
What's Fair? 86
What About Rules? 87
Choosing the Best 88
If You Were a King or Queen 90
When It's Dark Outside 91
Going to Church 93
Love Is . . . 95
How You Can Be a Star 96
Being a Christian 97
Knowing Jesus 100
Making Music 101
Why Pray? 103
What We All Can't Do 104
Grapevines and Branches 106
Why Be Sad? 108
Let's Talk About God 109
Your Sunday School 110
Names of God 112
Where Is Heaven? 113
What About Angels? 115

Let's Talk About Special Days

What Do You Like About Christmas? 119
Easter Eggs and Rabbits 120

Let's Talk About People

What Do You Eat? 125
Why Giving Is Better Than Receiving 126
Your Teachers 128
Keeping a Secret 130
Talking to Grandma and Grandpa 131
Cruel Children 134
Loving Children Who Are Different 136
People Who Get Angry 137
The Man Who Said "Thank You" 138
Is Honesty the Best Policy? 139
Children Singing 141
When People Play 142
The Fun of Giving 145
Wasters and Savers 146
Brothers and Sisters 147
Christians Who Run Out of Gas 149
Getting Even with Others 150
Heroes in the Bible 151
The Most Important Church Members 153
Friends 154
Liars and Lies 155
When Children Help 157
One of God's Helpers 159
Paintings and Painters 160
Having a Good Laugh 162

Index of Bible Passages 166
Topical Index 169
About the Author 175

A Personal Note from the Author

It seems to me that most adults aren't very good at carrying on conversations with children. Because of that, children usually talk much more readily with other children than with adults.

You see, it takes a desire to communicate, and many adults aren't eager to talk with children. But if children are to grow up in the grace of Christ, it's urgent that adults communicate with them. To communicate the Christian faith and life requires a planned focus on matters of Christian concern. And conversations need to be in the language and thinking of children.

This book is a resource designed to help adults explore matters of faith and life with children. It provides conversations that parents can have with their children at mealtime or bedtime or at any other suitable time. Sunday school teachers and pastors will find the readings to be a useful basis for children's devotions and sermons.

The entire chapters can be used for conversation, not just the questions. The comments and stories may be read as presented or spoken in the user's own words.

The readings are rich in Bible references. Depending on the age of the child, some of these can be memorized, making the Word of God an ongoing influence in the child's life. For older children a section has been added to show them where to read more about the topic in the Bible and ways to remember what they've learned.

Each conversation ends with a brief prayer, providing a closing response for the learner. The printed prayers do not end with "Amen," but are open to additions by the reader.

May this book be a blessing to both the adults and the children who engage in its conversations. Such talk will prove to be a life-giving joy to all involved.

ALLAN HART JAHSMANN

LET'S TALK ABOUT
YOU

Are You a Bossy Person?

A bossy person tries to be a boss. Do you know what that means? When people say, "You're the boss," they are saying that you may have your way. Bossy people usually want their own way. So what do you think bossy people often do?

- Do you like bossy people? Why, or why not?
- How do you feel when someone bosses you around?
- What do you do when someone bosses you?

A boy named Bert was bossy. He was always telling people what to do—even his parents. "Mom, bring me my shoes," he would yell in the morning. Or he'd say, "Hurry up and get me some breakfast." "OK, Buster," his mother would say, but that only made Bert more bossy. Why?

- Do you ever get bossy?
- What makes children bossy?

Some grownup people are bossy too. They like telling others what to do. Maybe that's because their parents let them be bossy when they were young.

Jesus was never bossy. He was kind. The Bible tells us to be kind to others, like Jesus was.

- Why doesn't a kind person try to be bossy?
- What does a kind person do instead?
- What kind of loving and helpful things do you do?

The next time you're bossy, remember that God wants you to be loving and kind as He is. That includes forgiving people when they're bossy.

▼ ▼ ▼

Bible Verse
Be kind to one another. Ephesians 4:32 (HBC)

For Older Children
You can read more about how God wants us to get along together in Ephesians 4:2-3.

Let's Pray
Dear Jesus, make me as kind to others as You are to me. Help me not to be bossy and make me more willing to let others have their way.

What If You Couldn't Remember Anything?

Can you remember a time you said, "I don't remember"? Sometimes you may not have wanted to remember, like when asked if you had done your homework or made your bed. Why don't you want to remember some things?

At other times you really forgot. Older people often forget things. They forget what they're told. They may even forget their own name.

Remembering is something your mind does for you. What would happen if your mind stopped remembering? Think of how lost you would get if you couldn't remember where you lived or who your parents were.

- If you had to choose what to remember, what would you choose?
- What would you like to forget?

In the Bible God says He will never forget us. Sometimes it seems as though God isn't with us, but that's because we sometimes forget that He's always with us and loves us.

There is one thing God forgets. Do you know what it is? God says He will forget the wrong things we do when we ask Him to forgive us. Because Jesus died for us on the cross, God is willing to forget what we do wrong. Why is that important to remember?

▼ ▼ ▼

Bible Verse
Remember your Creator while you are still young. Ecclesiastes 12:1 (TEV)

For Older Children
In Psalm 103 King David talks about how God forgives and forgets all our sin. Read the first five verses.

Let's Pray
Father in heaven, I know You will never forget me. Keep me from ever forgetting You and my Savior Jesus.

What's Your Name?

Whether you like your name or not, your name is important.

- What would your life be like if you didn't have a name?
- Without a name, what kinds of trouble would you have?

Some people's names say a lot about them. Remember the names of the dwarfs in the story of Snow White? If your name were Sleepy or Grumpy, what would people think? Soon you might become what your name said you were. A girl whose name was Sunny became a cheerful girl. She tried to be what her name said she was.

No matter what your name is, it tells who you are. It also stands for what you are and do. When you like what you are and do, you like seeing your name on what you've done. Why is that?

The Bible says God gave Jesus a name that is more important than any name anybody else ever had or will have. The name Jesus says He is our Savior. He saves people from their sins.

Some people say the name Jesus without caring about Him. They say His name when they're angry or scared. But people who love Jesus honor His name and worship Him.

- What are some other names for Jesus?
- How can you honor Jesus' name?

People who love Jesus are called *Christians*. They're called Christians because one of Jesus' other names is *Christ*. Christians also have another name. They are called children of God, because Jesus makes us God's children.

- What's wonderful about being a child of God?

▼ ▼ ▼

Bible Verse
In Christ Jesus you are all children of God. Galatians 3:26 (NRSV)

For Older Children
Read Luke 9:46-48 and tell someone what it says.

Let's Pray
Lord Jesus, I'm glad I'm called a Christian because that says I'm one of God's children.

Knowing the Right Time

Time is very important. Do you know how to tell what time it is?

- What time is it now?
- How do most people know the time?
- What would happen if no one knew what time it was?

There's a saying that says, "time waits for no one." Another says, "time marches on." What do these sayings tell us? "You can't stop the clock" is another saying. What does time do even when someone stops the clock?

Children often forget what time it is. They don't think about the time, especially when they're having fun. But forgetting what time it is can get you into trouble. Have you ever stayed out playing past the time you were told to come home?

Sometimes we can get into trouble by forgetting the wrong time to do something. Amanda and Molly were whispering back and forth to each other and giggling. They weren't paying attention to what Mrs. Jones, their teacher, was saying to them. Suddenly Mrs. Jones stopped talking and walked over to Amanda and Molly.

- Why was Mrs. Jones upset with Amanda and Molly?
- Is it always wrong to whisper and laugh in school?

The Bible says there's a right time for everything. God has a right time for whatever He does. He wants us to do things at the right time too. So even though it's fun to laugh with your friends, it's not the right time when you should be listening to your teacher.

It's always the right time to get to know God. You can know God by getting to know Jesus and learning to love Him.

▼ ▼ ▼

Bible Verse
He [God] has set the right time for everything. Ecclesiastes 3:11 (TEV)

For Older Children
Make a list of right times and a list of wrong times to do things.

Let's Pray
Lord God, help me to know the right time for the things I do.

What Do You Want to Be?

"What do you want to be when you grow up?" That's a question older people often ask young children. When they're very young a lot of children answer, "An airplane pilot or a fireman or what my daddy is."

■ What do you want to be when you grow up?

Some parents want their children to become ministers or doctors or teachers. But there are a lot of other jobs that need to be done too. What are some other jobs you could do when you grow up?

■ Why do people need plumbers?
■ How about police and firefighters?
■ What other kinds of workers do we need?

A good car repair person is very important. What would happen if no one could fix cars? Some children want to become

good athletes when they grow up. How would you like to become a famous baseball player or a tennis player who travels and plays all over the world?

No matter what you decide to do, you'll be able to do it for God. And you'll be able to do it the way God wants you to do it. Whatever you do, God wants you to do your very best, and He wants you to do it to help other people.

▼ ▼ ▼

Bible Verse
Whatever you do, work at it with all your heart, as though you were working for the Lord. Colossians 3:23 (TEV)

For Older Children
Make a list of what you may do to help other people when you grow up.

Let's Pray
Lord Jesus, whatever I do and try to become, help me do it for You.

Remembering What You Promised

Do you remember a time you said, "I promise"? What were some promises you made?

People make promises all the time. At the beginning of a new year people make a lot of promises. They call these promises *resolutions*.

- Have you ever made a New Year's resolution? What was it?
- Did you keep your promise?

It's sad but people who make promises often break them. Children who promise to be nice don't become nicer. By promising to be better they often get worse. How can you be sure to keep your promises and do the good things you want to do?

The Bible tells us a way that really works. It says that if you admit what you do wrong—like breaking your promises—and ask God to forgive you, then you become a different person. You stop doing what you're really sorry you've been doing. And you start doing what God wants you to do.

- What are some things you are sorry about?
- How can you ask God to forgive you?

Remember, if you ask God to forgive you, He will. As you start doing what God wants you to do, you'll start keeping your promises.

▼ ▼ ▼

Bible Verse
Every one of God's promises is a "Yes." 2 Corinthians 1:20 (NRSV)

For Older Children
Read 1 John 1:9 in your Bible and see what God promises to do for you.

Let's Pray
Dear God, I admit that I sin often and don't always keep my promises. Please forgive me for Jesus' sake and help me do what I say I will do.

Your Bag of Gifts

Almost everybody knows what a gift is. We usually think gifts come wrapped in a package. But some of God's best gifts are people.

So *you* are a gift from God. God gave you to your parents. You can also be a gift to a lot of other people.

- How can you be a gift to others?
- Who are some of the people you think are gifts to you?

Besides *being* a gift, every person has a *bag* of gifts to give to others. When you love others and do things for them, that's like giving them a gift.

What are some of the gifts you have in your bag?

- A happy smile?
- A loving heart?
- The ability to play an instrument?
- What can you do well?

Most children have the gift of making other people happy.

- What are some ways you can make others happy?
- What can you do for your parents?
- What can you do for other children?

The best gift God ever gave to make us happy is His Son, Jesus.

- Have you received God's gift of Jesus and His love?
- How can you give that gift to others?

▼ ▼ ▼

Bible Verse
Every good gift and every perfect present comes from heaven.
James 1:17 (TEV)

For Older Children
In Ephesians 4:11-12 you can read about some of the gifts God
gives people.

Let's Pray
Lord Jesus, fill my life with Your love so I'll have many gifts to
give to others.

The Best Use of Your Time

In a movie called *Dead Poets' Society*, a teacher told his students
to "Seize the day!" *Seize* means grab.

- What was the teacher telling his students to do with
  their time?

A young man named Jonathan decided to live each day as
though it might be his last day. What do you think he did?
Some children with leukemia get to choose one thing they'd like
to do before they die. They get to go to Disneyland or on a
cruise or on a trip to Hawaii or whatever.

- What would you do if you thought you had only one
  month left to live on earth?
- What do you think would be the *best* use of your time?

The Bible talks about making good use of the time we have.
It says, *now is the time* to live with God. This is also the time
God is willing to help us live the way He wants us to live.

■ What are some things God wants you to do?

▼ ▼ ▼

Bible Verse
Make good use of every opportunity you have. Ephesians 5:16
(TEV)

For Older Children
Write a plan to help you make the best use of tomorrow.

Let's Pray
Dear Jesus, show me how to make good use of every day You give me.

How Good Are Your Manners?

"Mind your manners," a mother told her little boy. He was acting silly at the dinner table.

■ What do you think he might have been doing?
■ What did the boy's mother mean when she told him to mind his manners?

Good manners are good behavior. When we have good manners we remember to say "please" and "thank you." We are kind to others and don't interrupt when they talk.

■ What are some other things that are good manners?
■ What would be some bad behavior?
■ What reasons do God's children have for using good manners?

A lot of children forget their manners when playing with

others. They push and shove each other and are rude. But it is possible to have fun and not be rough or mean.

- How do good manners give us more fun when we play?
- How do you think Jesus treated His friends?
- What kind of manners do you think Jesus had?

The friends of Jesus need to remember they are God's children. When you try to act like Jesus, you will have good manners. You won't talk nasty to others or try to hurt them. You won't be so loud that you upset people. Why not?

▼ ▼ ▼

Bible Verse
Remember . . . what you were taught and what you heard. Revelation 3:3 (TEV)

For Older Children
In Philippians 2:14-15 you can read more about how God wants you to act. Look up the verses in your Bible and maybe memorize them.

Let's Pray
Dear Jesus, Your love makes my behavior good and helps me to remember good manners. Please help me act like You.

Are You Ever Ashamed?

Some people think we should never be ashamed of what we do. Some children never are. They say, "It's okay" about everything they do, even wrong things.

Do you know what feeling ashamed means? It means

feeling badly because you've done something wrong or because you didn't do something good you could have done.

A group of boys cheated on a test at school. They weren't ashamed of what they had done. They were just sorry that the teacher caught them cheating. What reason did they have to be ashamed?

Some people are even proud of what they do wrong. They brag about it. On television one day there were people telling how they steal clothes and other things from stores. They thought they were smart because they could get away with it.

But people who love God and want to be like Him are sorry when they do wrong or when they don't do what is right. They know that Jesus died on a cross so they could have forgiveness. Because Jesus died for them, they love Him and don't want to do wrong. They feel very sorry when they do.

- Have you ever been ashamed of something you said or did?
- What can you say to God when you're ashamed?

The Bible says that when we are sorry and admit what we do wrong, God forgives us for Jesus' sake. He also helps us not to do wrong.

▼ ▼ ▼

Bible Verse
I am sorry for my sin. Psalm 38:18 (NRSV)

For Older Children
King David was very sorry when he sinned. You can read about how he was ashamed in Psalm 51.

Let's Pray
Lord God, I'm sorry for all I've done wrong. Please forgive me for Jesus' sake and help me to live the kind of life Jesus wants me to live.

What Scares You?

People are afraid of many different things. Some children are afraid of dogs. Others are afraid of snakes or rats. Some are afraid of being left alone, especially in a dark place.

- What are some things you're afraid of?
- Why are some people afraid to fly in an airplane?
- Why are some children afraid to ride a bicycle for the first time?

When people were scared, Jesus often told them, "Don't be afraid." Once the disciples were in a boat in the middle of a lake when there was a big storm. They looked out across the water and saw someone walking on the water toward them. They were afraid and thought it might be a ghost. But Jesus called out to them, "Don't be afraid!"

Jesus often said, "Don't be afraid" when He met people.

- Why were some people afraid of Jesus?
- No one needs to be afraid of Jesus. Why not?

There are some things you need to be afraid of. Like what? But when Jesus is with you, you don't need to be afraid. He will protect you and keep you safe from harm.

- What can you do to get help from Jesus when you're afraid?

■ Why can friends of Jesus feel safe?

▼ ▼ ▼

Bible Verse
He [God] will cover you with his wings; you will be safe in his care. Psalm 91:4 (TEV)

For Older Children
Make a list of things that frighten or worry you. Then crumple it up and throw it away.

Let's Pray
Dear God, whenever I'm afraid, please remind me that Jesus is with me and that I'm safe in His care.

Does Your Mother Work?

A lot of mothers with young children go to work at least some days every week. What happens at your house if your mother goes to work in the morning? Who makes your breakfast? What happens if your mother works at night? Who helps you with your schoolwork? Who says bedtime prayers with you and reads to you?

■ How do you feel about your mother working?
■ Did you ever ask her why she's working?
■ What did she say?

Maybe your mother has to work because she's a single parent and has to earn money. Maybe she's doing it to help you have things you couldn't have otherwise. There are lots of things you can do to show your mother you love her because she's working to help take care of you. You can help out at home or send her a note at work telling her how much you appreciate her.

- What can you do to help your mother when you're at home?
- What will make her life with you happier?
- What are some ways you can spend special time together?

In the Bible God gave a man named Moses some rules. We call them the Ten Commandments. They're in the Bible for all of us to obey. One of them tells us to *honor* our father and our mother.

Do you know what the word "honor" means? It means to love and do things for your parents and to remember that they are your parents and deserve your respect. All good parents love their children and do many good things for them. What do you do for your parents?

▼ ▼ ▼

Bible Verse
Honor your father and your mother. Exodus 20:12 (HBC)

For Older Children
Look up Exodus 20:12 to see what God promises those who honor their parents.

Let's Pray
Lord Jesus, You loved and honored Your parents. Help me do the same.

Why Not Admit It?

Jennifer and Peter were arguing because Peter had broken her new doll. "I didn't do it," said Peter. "Yes, you did," Jennifer insisted. "No, I didn't!" Peter yelled. "Yes, you did!" Jennifer yelled back. On and on it went.

Even when we know we're wrong, sometimes it's hard to admit it. Peter knew he had broken the doll. Jennifer knew it too. Why didn't Peter admit he was wrong?

- Why do you think it's hard to say you've done something wrong?
- When are you willing to say you did something wrong?

Sometimes we're afraid to admit we did wrong because we're afraid that others will get angry with us or maybe not like us anymore. It can be scary to admit we've done wrong. But the Bible says that if we admit it when we do wrong and are sorry, God will forgive us. So will people who love us.

- Have you ever admitted it when you did something wrong?

■ What happened when you said you were sorry—like when you broke something or forgot to do something or you hurt somebody?

The Bible says, "If we confess our sins to God . . . he will forgive us our sins." So why not admit what you do wrong? It's nice to be forgiven.

▼ ▼ ▼

Bible Verse
If we confess our sins to God . . . he will forgive us our sins. 1 John 1:9 (TEV)

For Older Children
In Psalm 51 King David asked God to forgive him for something bad he did. Read verses 10-11 and maybe memorize them.

Let's Pray
Dear Father in heaven, I know I have done many wrong things. Thank You for loving me anyway for Jesus' sake.

Your Worries and Fears
Older people sometimes think children don't have any worries and fears. They think they have to do all the worrying for them.

■ Have you ever worried about anything or been afraid of something?
■ What do you worry about?

Kevin was a young boy who worried that he was going to die soon. He worried about it so much that he couldn't sleep.

When he did sleep, he had nightmares. He dreamed he was in a coffin with the lid down and couldn't get out.

Kevin was afraid to talk about his dreams to anyone. He thought his parents might scold him or laugh at what he told them. So he kept his worry to himself, and that made him feel sick.

- When you worry or are afraid, do you usually tell someone about it or do you keep it to yourself?
- Why is it better to talk to someone about your worries and fears?
- Even if your parents or friends won't listen to you, who is always around and willing to listen to you?

A girl named Susan was afraid to be alone. She was even afraid to go to the bathroom alone in her own house. She was afraid that she might not be able to get out. When Susan's mother told her about Jesus, what do you think she said about Him?

The Bible says we should give all of our worries to God. He understands our worries and is big and strong enough to take care of them.

- How can you give your worries to God the next time you feel anxious or afraid?

▼ ▼ ▼

Bible Verse
Throw all your . . . worries on God because he cares for you. 1 Peter 5:7 (HBC)

For Older Children
In Mark 7:25-30 there is a story about a woman who begged

Jesus to heal her sick daughter. You can read what happened when you look up the verses in your Bible.

Let's Pray
Dear Jesus, I'm sorry that I worry when I don't need to. Remind me to give my worries to God because He loves and cares for me.

Wishing

Everybody wishes things. Have you ever made a wish and blown out candles on a birthday cake? Wishing is wanting something to come true. Lots of people wish to be rich or famous. Other people wish to have lots of thing—like toys. Some people wish they were someone else.

- What are some of the things you've wished for?
- Have any of your wishes ever come true?

Some wishing can be good. When he was a young man, President Clinton wished to become the president of our country—and he did. Because it was something he wished for and wanted very badly, he worked hard to make his wish come true.

But sometimes wishing can be bad—like wishing for something that's bad for us, or spending all our time wishing and dreaming instead of working or doing what we should. When we wish all of the time, we stop being happy with what we already have.

The apostle Paul wrote parts of the Bible. He said, "I have learned to be content [satisfied] with whatever I have." Paul let God decide what he was to be and do. He also said that he wanted to become what God wanted him to be. More than anything, Paul wished to be like Jesus.

Wishing doesn't always make something happen, but it will help to make it happen. Wishing to be like Jesus is always a good thing to wish for.

▼ ▼ ▼

Bible Verse
I have learned to be content [satisfied] with whatever I have. Philippians 4:11 (NRSV)

For Older Children
What do you want to be when you grow up? How would wishing help to make it come true?

Let's Pray
Lord God, I wish I could be more like Jesus. Other than that, please make me happy with whatever I am and have.

How Bright a Light Are You?

Jesus said He is the light of the world. He is the Savior who saves people from living in darkness. He gives people everywhere in the world the love of God and brightens their lives.

Jesus wants His friends to be lights too, and they are. When Jane wanted other children to see how loving Jesus is, she told them how He had died for the whole world. She also told them that He always forgives the people who ask Him for forgiveness and promises to answer their prayers.

The loving things we do are also like lights. They brighten people's lives and make them happy.

- How can you be a light and show others God's love by what you tell them?
- What things could you *do* to shine like a light?

In a song you may know, children sing, "This little light of mine, I'm gonna let it shine." When singing the song, children usually hold up a finger. But holding up a finger doesn't make any light.

- What do you have to do to shine like a light?
- How can you make your light shine brighter?

▼ ▼ ▼

Bible Verse
Let your light shine so people will see the good things you do and will praise your Father in heaven. Matthew 5:16 (HBC)

For Older Children
Make a list of the things you will do this week that will show others the love of Jesus.

Let's Pray
Dear Jesus, please let Your love shine through whatever I do.

Will You Forgive Me?

In the Lord's Prayer Jesus taught us to say, "Forgive us our trespasses (our sins) as we forgive those who sin against us."

When someone does something mean to you, it's much better to forgive them instead of wanting to get even. When we sin, God forgives us instead of getting even. He forgives us for Jesus' sake. And Jesus expects us to forgive others.

- How will we forgive others if we want God to forgive us?
- What are we asking God to do if we're not willing to forgive others?

Everybody loved Mary Ann. She was so nice. When anybody pushed her in the school yard, she'd smile and say, "That's all right. I forgive you." She did that because she knew Jesus wanted her to do it.

Be glad that God loves and forgives you for Jesus' sake. He died on a cross for all of us so we could have forgiveness. That's the good news called the gospel. When we forgive others, we love like God loves us.

▼ ▼ ▼

Bible Verse
In him [Jesus] we have . . . the forgiveness of our trespasses. Ephesians 1:7 (NRSV)

For Older Children
This week count the number of times you forgive others.

Let's Pray
Dear God, help me to forgive others the way You forgive me.

You Can Be a Peacemaker

There's a lot of violence in our country. Do you know what violence is? Violence is what people do to hurt others. Violence is fighting, hitting, stabbing, shooting, smashing, burning, or bombing.

But let's talk about peace—the peace of the Lord Jesus.

God gives this kind of peace to His people. It's the opposite of violence.

- What do you think peace is?
- What do I mean when I say, "Let's have peace" or "Let's make peace"?

People who are peacemakers try to get along with others. They also try to help others get along with one another. Sally was just a young girl, but she was always asking her parents to be nice to each other. She also tried to get along with her brother and sister.

Peace is also a feeling. It's a good feeling that you get when you're friendly and nice to others.

- What other feelings do people have when they feel peaceful?

Jesus gives peace to people. He loves and forgives us when we do wrong and helps us be kind and forgiving and friendly. And He wants all people to have peace and live in peace.

Jesus even died on a cross to give us peace. Be sure to ask Jesus for peace with God and all other people. And make peace with others. Jesus said peacemakers will be called children of God.

▼ ▼ ▼

Bible Verse
"Blessed are the peacemakers, for they will be called children of God." Matthew 5:9 (NRSV)

For Older Children
Try writing a story about a boy or girl who was a peacemaker.

Let's Pray
Thank You, Jesus, for giving me peace with God. Make me a peacemaker.

Avoiding Dangers

A sign on an old house said, "Danger-Keep Out." The windows in the house were smashed and some of the stairs going up to the front door were missing. Broken glass was all over the ground.

- Why did the house have a sign like that?
- What was dangerous about the house?

Sometimes signs along the highway say "Danger."

- What might be some dangers along a road?
- Why are people warned about dangers?

Whatever can harm us is a danger. Lots of things can be dangerous if you're not careful.

- What can you do to ride your bicycle safely?
- How can you make riding in a car safer?
- What are some other ways you can be safe from danger?

There's something else you can do to be safe from danger. A man named Martin Luther said that every morning you can ask God to send an angel to watch over you and keep you safe. You can do this by saying to God, "Send Your angel to be with me." Then be sure to thank God every evening for keeping you safe from danger.

▼ ▼ ▼

Bible Verse
His angel guards those who [love] the Lord and rescues them from danger. Psalm 34:7 (TEV)

For Older Children
Try drawing or painting your idea of an angel.

Let's Pray
Thank You, Lord, for having Your angel guard me and rescue me from dangers every day.

The Best Way to Be Rich

Ads on television sometimes promise to make you rich by showing you how to save or make money. Some people try to become rich by working hard or even by stealing. Why? What's so good about being rich?

The Bible warns us about loving money and things. It says loving money causes all kinds of evil. Evil is the opposite of what is good.

- Why do you think many people love money?
- What are some bad results that come from loving money?

There are lots of ways to be rich without having a lot of money. We can be rich in love when we love people and they love us. We can also be rich in having a lot of friends and good times. We can be rich in good works by doing nice things for other people. The apostle Paul said he made people rich by telling them about Jesus.

■ How does knowing Jesus make you rich even when
you don't have a lot of money?

God wants us to be rich in good works. That means God
wants us to do a lot of good things for others. By doing good
for others, we make them rich with love. We can make others
rich also by talking to them about Jesus. Knowing Him is
worth more than anything else in the world. That's the best way
to be rich.

▼ ▼ ▼

Bible Verse
They [the rich] are to do good, to be rich in good works, gen-
erous and ready to share. 1 Timothy 6:18 (NRSV)

For Older Children
Second Corinthians 8:9 tells how Jesus made us all rich. What
did He do? What does He give us?

Let's Pray
Dear Jesus, make me rich in doing good things for others. Help
me to make others rich by giving them Your love.

Why Go To School?

Most children go to school. First comes elementary school, then
middle school, then high school. After high school, you can
either begin working or go to another school called college. There
are still more schools after college—lawyers go to law school,
doctors go to medical school, and pastors go to seminary.

■ What kind of school do you go to?
■ Why do you go to school?

- What are some of the things you learn at school?
- What would happen if you didn't go to school at all?

School isn't the only place you can learn things. You can learn at home too—how to make your bed or how to help your mother do the dishes. You can learn at Sunday school too.

- What are some of the things you learn at home?
- What are some of the things you've learned at Sunday school?

We learn something every day. God is glad when we learn new things. He wants us to learn to do things for Him.

- What would you like to do for God?
- What do you know about God that you can teach others?

▼ ▼ ▼

Bible Verse
Grow in the grace and knowledge of our Lord and Savior Jesus Christ. 2 Peter 3:18 (NRSV)

For Older Children
Look up Luke 2:52. It's another verse that tells how Jesus grew up.

Let's Pray
Dear God, thank You for helping me to learn new things at school, at home, and at Sunday school. I want to learn how I can do things for You. Please help me to grow, especially in the love of my Savior Jesus Christ.

You and Your Parents

Our Lord Jesus loved His parents. He worked with His father, Joseph, who was a carpenter. He went to church with His parents. When He was hanging on a cross and suffering a lot of pain, He asked His friend John to take care of His mother Mary.

One of the commandments God had Moses give to His people long ago says, "Honor your father and your mother." The Bible repeats this command of God many times.

- How can you honor your parents?
- How do children benefit from loving and respecting their parents?
- What happens when children disobey their parents?

Christopher was a very unhappy boy. He never wanted to do what his parents told him to do. His mother often punished him, and his father sometimes spanked him.

Parents are a valuable gift from God. Imagine what your life would be without any parents. How would it be different from what it is?

- How can you thank God for giving you a home and parents who love you?

▼ ▼ ▼

Bible Verse
Children . . . obey your parents, for this is the right thing to do. Ephesians 6:1 (TEV)

For Older Children
The Bible tells about a son who caused a lot of trouble for his father, King David. His name was Absalom. In 2 Samuel 18:31-33 you can read what the king said when Absalom died.

Let's Pray
Lord God, thank You for giving me parents. Make me willing to obey my parents as Jesus obeyed His.

Learning Not to Grumble

Children are famous for many things. Can you guess what most of them do on a car trip? You're right—they complain. What do they complain about?

Some parents plan games for their children to play in the car.

- What kind of games do you like to play on a trip?
- What else might keep you from whining and complaining on a trip?

In the Bible the people of Israel complained a lot when they were traveling to a new home across a desert. God became angry over their whining. He said they weren't thankful for what He was doing for them.

Maybe you've heard about the Grumble Box. At the Smith's house the children were always grumbling and complaining. They grumbled when they were asked to do something. They complained when they didn't have anything to do.

One day Mrs. Smith said, "You know, we'd be happier if we didn't grumble so much. Here's a box with a hole in the top. Maybe we'll learn not to grumble if we all put a penny into the box whenever we complain."

The family agreed, so the box was put on the kitchen table. Whoever grumbled had to put a penny into the box. At the end of the month they counted the pennies. There were 213! That made them all laugh—and grumble less.

▼ ▼ ▼

Bible Verse
Do everything without complaining or arguing. Philippians 2:14
(TEV)

For Older Children
Each time you hear someone complain this week say, "God loves you" to that person. See what happens.

Let's Pray
Lord Jesus, keep me from being a whiner and complainer. That you are being with me is enough reason to be happy.

Bad Words and Good Words

Children sometimes say bad words. Some bad words are about bad things people do with each other. Some words wish that something bad would happen to others. They ask God to hurt people or things.

Some people say the name of Jesus or God without a good reason. They often yell the word "God" or "Jesus" when they're angry or upset. The Bible tells us we shouldn't use God's name in vain. That means we should never use it without a good reason.

- What are some *good* reasons to use the name of God or Jesus?

Swearing is something else the Bible tells us not to do. Some people say, "honest to God" or "by God I'll do it." That's another way of using God's name carelessly.

Jesus said, "Let your words simply be 'Yes, Yes' or 'No, No.'

Anything more than this is [wrong] (Matthew 5:37)." That's why people who love God do not want bad words to come out of their mouths.

▼ ▼ ▼

Bible Verse
You must not use the name of the Lord, your God, carelessly. Exodus 20:7 (HBC)

For Older Children
You can read more about the kinds of words we should and shouldn't say in Ephesians 4:29-31. Verse three tells you who gets upset when we do.

Let's Pray
Lord God, I know You want only good words to come out of my mouth. Keep me from speaking words that are bad.

How Brave Are You?
American Indians called their young fighters *braves*. They expected them to be brave.

■ Do you know what it means to be brave?

Some Indian tribes gave their young braves a test of courage. On his thirteenth birthday, a boy was blindfolded and led out of the camp during the night. Several miles from home his blindfold was removed and he was left in a dark forest. There he had to spend the night all by himself.

After staying awake all night, the boy would finally see the sun begin to appear above the trees. To his surprise, he would also see a man standing near him, armed with a bow and arrow. It was his father. His father had been there all night long.

- Do you think the boy was brave for staying out in the forest all night long?
- What do you think the father was doing there? Why?

Sometimes we all feel like those young braves felt in the dark—alone and afraid.

- When do you feel scared?
- What do you worry about?

Jesus told His friends, "I am always with you." So you don't ever have to be afraid. You're never alone, even when it's dark and you think no one is with you.

- Who is always with you?
- What can you do when you feel alone and afraid?
- How will you feel when you remember that Jesus is with you?

▼ ▼ ▼

Bible Verse
Jesus said, "I am always with you." Matthew 28:20 (HBC)

For Older Children
Psalm 91 is a poem about God's protection. Read verses 14-16.

Let's Pray
Dear Jesus, whenever I'm afraid remind me that You are always with me.

Good Reasons for Reading

- Do you know how to read?
- Do you like to read?

There are some people who can't read. They never learned how.

- How could you learn to read better?
- What is your favorite book?

Martin Luther said learning to know Jesus is the best reason for learning to read. What do you think? What other good reasons do people have for reading?

You can learn all kinds of things by reading. The library is full of books about many different subjects. There are books about games, books about history, books about the world, and books about anything else you can think of.

Reading is one way you can learn to know Jesus better. One of His friends named John wrote a book about Jesus. It's in the Bible. John wrote the book so you could get to know Jesus better. It tells all about Jesus' life on earth—the things He said and did.

- What are some Bible stories you've learned to know by reading them?
- What do you think is the best story in the Bible?
- Why is the story about Jesus so important?

▼ ▼ ▼

Bible Verse
These [words] have been written in order that you may believe that Jesus is the Messiah, the Son of God. John 20:31 (TEV)

For Older Children

You can find John's book about Jesus in the New Testament. Maybe you could start reading a little of it every day to learn more about Jesus.

Let's Pray

Dear Jesus, help me learn to read well so I can read the Bible and learn more about You and life with God.

A Happy Home

Almost everybody wants to live in a happy home. What do you think makes a home a happy place? What kind of home would you like to live in?

- What is something that your family does to make your home happy?
- What would make your home even happier?
- If you were a father or mother, what would you do to make your home a happy place?

Parents aren't the only ones who can make a home happy. Children can make a home happy too. Susan's mother called her Miss Sunshine because Susan smiled a lot and always tried to be cheerful.

- What other things can children do to make their home a happy place?
- How can children help their parents?

Jesus called God *our Father in heaven*. When God is our Father, we are His children. Best of all, when we are God's children, Jesus is our brother.

- In what ways is God like a good parent?
- Why is it nice to have Jesus as a brother?
- How does Jesus make a home a happy place?

▼ ▼ ▼

Bible Verse
Jesus said, "Whoever does what God wants him [or her] to do is my brother and sister and mother." Matthew 12:50 (NRSV, simplified)

For Older Children
You can read more about how brothers and sisters can make a happy home in Psalm 133.

Let's Pray
Dear Jesus, thank You for giving me a home. Help me to make my home a happy place and live with me.

Things You're Ready to Do

"When you're older," Tim's dad would often say to him. Tim always wanted to do things that he was too young to do. Tim wanted to drive a car and play outside after dark. He wanted to stay home without a babysitter and not go to bed until late.

- Would you like to drive a car?
- Why do most boys and girls want to drive a car?
- Why aren't children allowed to drive until they are older?

Imagine what would happen if children were allowed to drive cars. What do you think? They might not be able to see above the steering wheel or reach the pedals with their feet. A lot of bad accidents would happen.

The Bible says there's a right time for everything. There's a time to be born and a time to die, a time to be happy and a time to cry.

- Can you think of some things you're not ready to do?
- How about getting married? Are you ready for that?

But there are many things you can do before you're older.

- What are some things children can do?
- How old do you have to be to pray for others?
- What else can you do for others?

The next time you want to do something like drive a car or stay out after dark, think about the things you are old enough to do. The Bible says, "God has set the right time for everything" (Ecclesiastes 3:11, TEV).

▼ ▼ ▼

Bible Verse
Everything . . . will happen at its own set time. Ecclesiastes 3:17 (TEV)

For Older Children
You can read more about a right time for everything in Ecclesiastes 3:1-8.

Let's Pray
Dear God, I'm glad there's a right time for everything. Help me to know what the right time is.

Getting an Allowance

Some children get an allowance every week. Do you know what that is? Do you get an allowance? Don't tell how much. It's better to keep it a secret.

Even if you don't get some money from your parents every week, you probably get some for Christmas or on your birthday or to spend on a trip. The question to answer is "What do you do with what you get?"

Some children are expected to save at least a part of the money they receive. Others think they should spend whatever they get. They think the word "allowance" means they're allowed to do whatever they want to do with their money.

Everything we receive is a gift from God—even our allowance. God wants us to use what He gives us in good ways.

- What would be some good ways to use your money?
- What would be some bad ways to use your money?

The Bible says God loves people who share what they have. A person who shares is called a cheerful giver.

- Are you cheerful when you share your money or things with others?
- Why don't a lot of people want to share what they have?

Don't forget: God wants us all to share a part of what we have with others who need it.

- What are some ways you can share your allowance with others?

▼ ▼ ▼

Bible Verse
God loves a cheerful giver. 2 Corinthians 9:7 (NRSV)

For Older Children
Someone who *tithes* gives God 10 percent of what he or she receives from God. Try to find out how much that would be for you.

Let's Pray
Lord God, I know I don't always want to share what I have. Make me a cheerful giver.

Deciding Which Way to Go

A well-known poem says that a road a person was traveling suddenly went in two directions. For a long time the traveler looked down one of the ways, then took the other because it seemed less used. He thought that way would be more interesting.

Sometimes our life is called a journey, a trip to distant places. Often we come to a point where the road goes in two directions. Then we must decide whether to go to the right or to the left, down a crooked path or along a straight road.

■ How do you usually decide what to do when you have to make a choice?

Sometimes you have to make a choice between what you've been taught by your parents or church and what you want to do, even if you know it's wrong.

A group of David's friends tried to talk him into stealing some tapes from a music store. For a long time he wondered what to do. It seemed easy enough to steal them, but David's parents had taught him that stealing was wrong. At the same time, David wanted to do what his friends wanted him to do.

- What reasons did David have for stealing the tapes?
- What reasons did he have for *not* stealing them?
- What helped David make the right choice?

When you have to make a choice between what you know is right and what you want to do, you can ask God to help you do the right thing. He will.

▼ ▼ ▼

Bible Verse
You are my God; teach me to do your will. Psalm 143:10 (TEV)

For Older Children
Write your own prayer for God's help in making right choices.

Let's Pray
Lord God, You are my reason for choosing Your ways. Help me when I have to make difficult choices.

Taking Care of Your Pet

All night long Abby could hear a dog barking. It was cold outside and the dog next door had been left without a dog house or any other place to stay warm. The people he belonged to were on a trip for a few days. Abby worried that they hadn't left enough food and water for the poor dog left out in the cold.

Did you know that dogs have feelings just like children? They need lots of love and attention.

- How can you tell when a dog is happy?
- How can you tell when a dog is sad?

Animals, especially our pets, depend on us to take care of them. When we don't love them, they suffer. God wants us to be kind to animals as well as to people. Having a pet is a big responsibility.

- Do you have a pet? What kind?
- What's your pet's name?
- What kinds of things do you do for your pet?
- What does your pet do for you?
- What could you say to God for your pet?

Some churches have a special day for pets. On that day children bring their pets to church, and the pastor asks God to be good to the pets. What do you think of that idea?

▼ ▼ ▼

Bible Verse
A good person takes care of his animals. Proverbs 12:10 (HBC)

For Older Children
Make a poster that tells children how to take care of their pets.

Let's Pray
Dear God, please show me how to take good care of my pets.

What Do You Own?

"That's mine!" Trevor yelled. "That's mine!" He didn't want any of the other children to play with his toys at his birthday party.

"That's my room!" Susan said. "You can't go in there!" She didn't want her little brother to play in her room.

- Why do you think Trevor thought the toys belonged to him?
- Why did Susan think the room was hers?

A lot of people act as though they own things. To own something means that it belongs only to you and that you can do whatever you want with it.

- What are some things you think you own?
- How long will you get to keep the things you think you own?

The Bible says, "The earth is the Lord's and all that is in it." That means everything in the whole world belongs to God. He gives us some things to use for a little while, but He is the only one who gets to keep what we have. It all belongs to Him. We just get to use them for a while.

- How should you treat things when they don't belong to you?
- How will you use what you have when you know it all belongs to God?

We belong to God too. Jesus paid for us with His life when He died for us on the cross. He redeemed us. That means He bought us. When we remember that we belong to God, how will we want to act?

▼ ▼ ▼

Bible Verse
The earth is the LORD's and all that is in it. Psalm 24:1 (NRSV)

For Older Children
Make a list of some things you can do to help take care of God's world.

Let's Pray
Lord God, help me to remember I belong to You and everything I have is a gift from You.

If You Couldn't Hear
Some people are *deaf*. That means they can't hear. They can't hear what other people say to them, or the radio or music. Think of how different your life would be if you couldn't hear.

- If you couldn't hear, what are some of the sounds you would miss?
- What are some things you would have a hard time doing if you were deaf?

Some people who can't hear learn to *see* what others are saying by watching their lips. See if you can read someone's lips. Can you tell what they're saying? Other people get hearing aids that go in their ears to help them hear. Some deaf children learn to read what people say with their hands. That's called *sign language*.

Jesus said, "Whoever has ears to hear with ought to listen." He was saying, "If you can hear, be sure to listen to what I say." What Jesus said long ago is written in the Bible. We can hear what He says by listening to people who teach us about Him and what He said when He was on earth. What have you heard about Jesus?

We can show God that we're thankful for ears that can hear by listening to good things.

- What are some good things to listen to and enjoy?
- What are some things God doesn't want us to listen to?

Be glad that you can hear. Listen to beautiful and good things.

▼ ▼ ▼

Bible Verse
Whoever has ears to hear with ought to listen. Luke 8:8 (HBC)

For Older Children
What did the prophet Isaiah say King Hezekiah should be sure to hear? Look up 2 Kings 20:16 to find out.

Let's Pray
Thank you, Jesus, for ears that can hear. Teach me to listen to Your teachings and to enjoy the good sounds around me.

It's Fun to Work

"Why don't you come to work with me today?" Anne's dad said one morning. Her dad was a teacher at a college. His office had a big table and models of planes hanging from the ceiling. Anne liked to see his office and classroom and to meet the other teachers who worked at his school.

- Have you ever gone to work with your mom or dad?
- If you did, what did you do?

Some people hate to go to work. They don't like what they do. Other people enjoy their jobs and like to work. Most children like to work. They like to help wash the car, water the lawn, or paint whatever needs painting.

- What kind of work do you like to do?
- Why is it important to enjoy your job?
- What do you think happens to people who hate their jobs?

Did you ever watch how ants work? The Bible says we can learn how to work by watching ants.

- How do ants work?

Lazy people don't like to work. They'd rather sit around and be bored instead of doing work.

Jesus worked when He lived on earth. He said He wanted to do the work of His Father in heaven. Do you know what that was? He told people about God and taught them how to live with God. He also made sick people well.

God wants us to enjoy working when we can. It's a way of helping others. How can you help others by working?

▼ ▼ ▼

Bible Verse

Lazy people should learn a lesson from the way ants live. Proverbs 6:6 (TEV)

For Older Children

Make a list of jobs. Put circles around those you'd enjoy doing.

Let's Pray

Dear Jesus, make me glad to work when I can. Keep me from being lazy.

A Good Heart

Your heart pumps blood to all parts of your body. If your heart stops doing its work, you can get very sick and your body can die. It's very important to keep your heart healthy and strong.

Do you know how to make your heart strong? One way is to eat healthy food and not eat a lot of fatty foods, like French fries or potato chips. Another way is to exercise every day.

- What are some good, healthy foods?
- Which healthy foods are your favorites?
- What kinds of exercises do you like to do?

There's another kind of heart that keeps people alive and healthy. You can't hear this heart thumping like the one that pumps blood, but you can see it in the way people act. When people say "Have a heart," they want you to feel and act loving and kind and helpful.

Your loving heart needs food and exercise too. Jesus is the food that gives you a loving heart. You can exercise this heart by learning the Bible and getting to know Jesus well.

- How will Jesus give you a good heart?
- What are some other ways you can make your loving heart healthy and strong?

▼ ▼ ▼

Bible Verse
People look at the outside appearance, but the Lord looks at the heart. 1 Samuel 16:7 (HBC)

For Older Children
In 1 Samuel 16:6-13 you can read how God looked at King David's heart.

Let's Pray
Lord God, give me a heart that is kind and good, through Jesus my Savior.

Being a Good Sport

The word "sport" has lots of different meanings. A boy named Nick had a dog named Sport. He was called Sport because he was a good sport.

What does it mean to be a good sport? Nick's sister says "Be a good sport" when she wants him to do something her way. To her, being a good sport means doing what she wants.

Sport is also a word for some kinds of games and activities.

- What kinds of sports do you like to play?

Being a good sport when playing sports is very important. Being a good sport means playing by the rules and being honest and fair.

- What kind of player is a poor sport?
- What happens when someone tries to win a game by cheating or not following the rules?

The next time someone tries to win a game by lying or cheating, you can say, "You're not being a good sport. God wants us to be good sports and do what is right."

▼ ▼ ▼

Bible Verse
It is foolish to enjoy doing wrong. Proverbs 10:23 (TEV)

For Older Children
Write a little story about someone who was either a good sport or a poor sport. You can draw pictures to help tell the story. Read it to someone when you've finished.

Let's Pray
Lord God, make me a good sport and keep me from doing wrong.

Who Are Your Heroes?

There's a story called *The Great Stone Face*. It's about a young man who lived near the mountains. On the side of one of the mountains was something that looked like a face. The young man thought the face looked nice and kind, so he spent lots of time looking at it. Gradually the young man began to look like that face.

When we spend a lot of time around someone or want to be like him or her, we become more and more like that person. That's why it's important to choose good heroes. Heroes are people we admire and want to imitate.

- Who are some of your heroes?
- What do you like about them?

Sometimes we get our heroes from books or television. What a person likes to read or watch tells a lot about that person.

Michael's favorite television program has lots of fighting in it. His hero isn't very nice and says lots of bad words. Michael fights with other children at school and often gets in trouble for saying bad words.

- Why do you think Michael fights and says bad words?
- Is Jesus one of your heroes?

There has never been a more wonderful person than Jesus. He is God's Son and just like God. The Bible tells us to grow up to be like Jesus. If Jesus is your hero, you'll grow up to be kind and good like Him.

▼ ▼ ▼

Bible Verse
We must grow up in every way . . . into Christ. Ephesians 4:15 (NRSV)

For Older Children
Check John 13:35 to see how you can become like Jesus.

Let's Pray
Dear God, I want to grow up to be like Jesus. Please help me.

Let's See Your Teeth

Some children show their teeth a lot because they like to smile. Other children don't show their teeth very much because they don't like to smile.

Teeth are a wonderful gift from God. Without them, you couldn't chew your food or chew gum. God knew that people needed teeth to chew, so He gave them to us. Did you ever thank God for your teeth?

- How would you look if you had no teeth?
- How would you feel?

Some older people have no teeth or very few teeth. People without teeth often get false teeth to help them chew their food. Children sometimes have missing teeth.

- Have you lost any teeth?
- Why do some people's teeth fall out?

When we have teeth, we need to take good care of them so they'll last a long time. You can help take care of your teeth by brushing them. You can also take care of your teeth by going to the dentist. Have you ever been to a dentist?

- What do you do to keep your teeth nice and white?
- How often do you brush them?
- What gives people cavities?
- How do dentists fix teeth?

The next time your dentist fixes and cleans your teeth, say a "thank you" to God for dentists. Remember to thank your dentist too.

▼ ▼ ▼

Bible Verse
In all your prayers ask God for what you need, always asking him with a thankful heart. Philippians 4:6 (TEV)

For Older Children
Psalm 117 is a short poem that tells all people to praise God for His love and blessing. Look it up in your Bible. You may want to memorize it.

Let's Pray
Thank You, God, for giving me teeth and for dentists who help me take care of them.

LET'S TALK ABOUT
GOD'S WORLD

When It Snows

Does it snow where you live? Some people don't like it when there's lots of snow and their car gets stuck in it. But most children *love* snow. They like skiing and sledding and throwing snowballs and making a snowman.

- What do you like most about snow?
- How does the snow make you feel?
- Why does everything look pretty when it's covered with snow?

The Bible says that when God loves and forgives us, we become whiter than snow. All the bad things we do get covered with God's love. That makes us look as pure and pretty as snow.

- How do you feel when you think about God's love covering you like snow covers trees?
- How can you enjoy God's love every day?

▼ ▼ ▼

Bible Verse
The Lord says, ". . . I wash you as clean as snow." Isaiah 1:18 (TEV)

For Older Children
Try drawing a picture of something covered with snow—maybe yourself or a snowman.

Let's Pray
Father in heaven, please forgive all my sins and make me whiter than snow.

Whatever God Has Made

God has made many wonderful things. Have you ever noticed how beautiful flowers are?

- Do you know the names of some of the flowers?
- What are your favorites?
- What colors do flowers come in?

Animals are wonderful to look at too. A little puppy is so nice to hold. A horse is also very interesting.

- How does a horse show that she or he likes you?
- What do horses do when they're happy to be outdoors?

Birds don't just fly around in circles. Sometimes they sit on the top of a tree and let the tree swing them. Geese like to follow each other in the air, "tooting their horns." Chickens are birds too, but they usually stay on the ground.

- Which birds do you like the most?
- Why?

Do you know how flowers and animals and birds became so wonderful? God made them the way they are. He made all kinds of flowers and animals and birds. They're all different.

And do you know the most wonderful of all the creatures God has made? People. In the Bible a poet wrote, "I praise you [God], for I am . . . wonderfully made. Wonderful are your works."

Take a good look at your body. See what it can do. It's wonderfully made. Then tell God what you think of your body.

▼ ▼ ▼

Bible Verse
I praise you [God]. . . . Wonderful are your works. Psalm 139:14 (NRSV)

For Older Children
In Psalm 139:1-6 you can read about how God made you.

Let's Pray
Lord God, all the things You have made are wonderful. I can never praise You enough for all You have made.

Learning From Geese

Every year, when the weather begins to get cold, groups of geese begin to fly to places where the weather is warmer. Have you ever seen them? They fly together in the shape of a V, with one bird in front, then two or three, then four or five, and so on.

Do you know why geese fly together the way they do? Because the flapping of their wings separates the air for the birds behind them and makes it easier for the birds to fly. When the goose up front gets tired, she lets another bird fly up and take her place.

Have you ever heard geese when they fly? The geese make a noise called honking. It sounds like a horn. By honking the geese tell those ahead of them to keep going. When a goose gets tired or sick or wounded and has to quit flying, two other geese follow the sick goose down to help her. They stay with the goose until she is able to fly again.

God wants us to do for others what geese do for other geese.

- What can you learn from geese?
- How can you help other children?
- Would you stay with someone who needed your help?

Remember, Jesus died on the cross to give us life with God. That's the most anyone could ever do for us.

▼ ▼ ▼

Bible Verse
Christ died for everyone, so that those who live would no longer live for themselves. 2 Corinthians 5:15 (HBC)

For Older Children
In Luke 6:31 Jesus gave us a good rule to follow. It's called the Golden Rule. Try to memorize it.

Let's Pray
Lord Jesus, even geese help each other. Make me ready to help other people in whatever ways I can.

Wonders in the World
There are many wonders in God's world. Niagara Falls is a huge waterfall and is one of the great wonders of the world. A big cave in New Mexico is wonderful. It's called the Carlsbad Caverns. Volcanoes that explode and shoot melted rock into the sky make us wonder how it can happen. High mountains and large deserts and big oceans are all wonders.

- What's a place you thought was wonderful?
- What made it seem wonderful to you?

What's wonderful about the sky? The clouds? The sun and

the moon? How about the way the sky looks in the morning— or in the evening?

A man in the Bible said there were four things he thought were wonderful: the way an eagle flies in the sky, the way a snake lies on a rock, the way ships sail on water, and the way boys and girls act when they're in love. Why do you think he thought those things were wonderful?

All of the things God made are wonderful—from the great whales in the ocean to the tiniest bugs. Even more wonderful is a little baby.

You and I are wonderfully made by God. But who do you think was the most wonderful person who ever lived? Yes, His name is Jesus. Long before He was born the Bible said Jesus would be called Wonderful. Do you know why? Because He was God Himself.

▼ ▼ ▼

Bible Verse
He [Jesus] will be called "Wonderful. . . ." Isaiah 9:6 (TEV)

For Older Children
You can read about the things the man found wonderful in Proverbs 30:18-19.

Let's Pray
Lord Jesus, everything God made is wonderful, but nothing is as wonderful as You.

The Gifts of Food and Water

Food and water may not be free, but they are gifts from God. We all need food and water to survive. Without them we would die. Even though food and water are so important, we often take them for granted. Maybe we don't think about our food and water enough.

- Where does food come from?
- Where does water come from?
- Where did people get food before there were grocery stores?
- What would we have to do if we couldn't get water from our faucets?

Animals need food and water too. Almost all baby animals and birds get their food from their parents.

- How are children kept alive when they are young?
- What do animals feed their babies?

God makes most parents willing to give their children food when they are young. Have you ever thanked God for that?

In a prayer called "The Lord's Prayer" Jesus taught us to ask God for daily bread. Daily bread means the food we need every day and whatever we need to stay alive, including water. God gives us food and water in many ways.

When you sit down for your meals, remember to thank God for giving you food to eat and water to drink every day.

▼ ▼ ▼

Bible Verse
He [the Lord God] . . . gives food to the hungry. Psalm 146:7 (TEV)

For Older Children
You can read the entire Lord's Prayer in Matthew 6:9-13.

Let's Pray
Lord God, thank You for giving me food every day.

Bird Nests and Little Birds

Have you ever seen a little bird's nest? Did you notice how wonderfully they're put together? The mother bird collects all kinds of things to make her nest: string, twigs, fluffy cotton, and much more. Often she builds her nest high up in a tree where other animals can't get to it.

Soon after her nest is made, little eggs appear. Where do you think they come from? Why does the mother bird sit on the eggs?

When baby birds first come out of the eggs, they are helpless. They can't see or fly. So the mother bird has to feed them.

- Have you ever seen a mother bird feed her babies?
- How does she feed them?
- What else does the mother bird do for her baby birds?

In some ways God is like a mother bird. He gave us a safe place to live when we were babies and gave us parents to feed us. Like a mother bird God watches over us and keeps dangers away.

Jesus once told His friends to look at the birds and see how happy they are. They sing and play and don't worry. And God gives them the food they need. How does He do that?

The Bible also says God takes us up high on His wings, like some birds take their children, and teaches us how to fly. How do you think God does that?

▼ ▼ ▼

Bible Verse
You are worth so much more than birds. Luke 12:24 (HBC)

For Older Children
In Matthew 6:25-26 you can read what Jesus said about God's care of birds. Look it up in your Bible.

Let's Pray
Lord God, I'm glad You think I'm worth much more than a bird. Thank You for sending Jesus to make me one of Your children.

Going to Faraway Places

Some Sunday newspapers have a travel section every week. It describes and shows places where people go on vacation. They go to faraway countries and to places in their own country where they haven't been.

- Why do people like to travel?
- What do they like about going on a trip?
- Do you like to travel? Why or why not?

People who travel learn a lot about God and the world He made. Every part of the world is different and shows us how creative God is to have made such wonderful places.

- If you traveled all the way around the world, what are some of the things you would see?
- What would you *like* to see?

Jesus didn't go to faraway countries when He was a young man, but He did travel to many places in Israel, the country where He lived. When Jesus traveled, He went to different places to teach the people about God, His Father in heaven.

Some people go and live in faraway countries to teach others about God. They are called *missionaries*. Even though missionaries live far away, you can help them teach others about God by praying for them or sending them money.

Maybe someday you'll be able to go to a faraway place to help people learn to know and love Jesus.

▼ ▼ ▼

Bible Verse
"Therefore go to people everywhere in the world and make them my disciples." Matthew 28:19 (HBC)

For Older Children
The apostle Paul was a missionary for Jesus. You can read about some of his travels to faraway places in Acts 13:1-14.

Let's Pray

Lord Jesus, even if I don't get to faraway places, make me willing to help faraway people learn to know and love You.

When It Rains

Do you know the song that says, "Rain, rain, go away. Come again some other day"? There's another song about rain that says, "I love to hear the patter of the raindrops." How do you feel about rain?

- Do you like rain? Why or why not?
- What's your favorite thing to do on a rainy day?

The Bible says God sends the rain. It's a gift to us. Farmers need rain. Without the rain their wheat or corn shrivels up. Without rain people would run out of water to drink.

Sometimes there's lots of rain. When there's too much rain, it causes floods. Rivers get so full of water they overflow. Do you know the story of Noah and the big flood? It rained for forty days and nights, and the whole world was covered with water.

But God saved Noah and his family. They lived in a big houseboat with all kinds of animals until the water went away.

After that flood God put a rainbow in the sky. The rainbow was God's promise that He would never again cover all the land with water. So even though it may rain and rain, we know there will never be a flood as big as Noah's again.

- Have you ever seen a rainbow?
- What did it look like?

The next time there's a rainy day, thank God that He sends

the rain to help things grow. Also thank God that He sends the rainbow to remind us of His promise.

▼ ▼ ▼

Bible Verse
He [God] gives you rain from heaven. Acts 14:17 (TEV)

For Older Children
You can read about Noah and the big flood in Genesis 6:5-8 and 7:11-24.

Let's Pray
Dear Father in heaven, thank You for the rain, the water that keeps Your world alive.

LET'S TALK ABOUT
JESUS AND GOD

How to Say "Thanks"

Children sometimes forget to say "thank you." Parents remind their children to thank the people who do things for them. Adults are pleased when children say "thank you," especially when they say it without being told to do so.

- Why do parents make such a big deal about saying "thank you"?
- Why is saying "thank you" very important?

The Bible often tells us to say thanks to God for all He does for us and gives to us. It makes God happy when we thank Him.

- What has God done for you?
- What are some of the things God does for you every day?
- What's the best thing God has done for you?

It's important to say "thank you" because it shows that we are thankful.

- How does being thankful make you feel?
- How does saying "thank you" make the person you're thanking feel?

When you forget to say thanks, the people who do things for you sometimes wish they hadn't. They may stop doing those nice things. So remember to say "thank you" when people do nice things for you. It's a very good habit.

▼ ▼ ▼

Bible Verse
How good it is to give thanks to you, O LORD. Psalm 92:1 (TEV)

For Older Children
Psalm 92:1-5 gives you some ways to say thanks to God. Look it up in your Bible.

Let's Pray
Lord God, make me a thankful person who also says thanks for Your gifts and blessings.

What's Fair?

"That's not fair!" Mark shouted when he didn't get a turn to bat the ball with his friends.

- When someone says, "That's not fair," what do they mean?
- Did you ever hear someone say, "That's not fair" or "You're not being fair"?
- What made him or her say that?

Many times it's easy to see what isn't fair. If we're playing a game and I cheat, why isn't that fair? If you steal what doesn't belong to you, why isn't that fair? If you were sharing some candy with two other children, what would be fair? What wouldn't be fair?

God is always fair in everything He does. He treats all people better than they deserve to be treated. He is good to all, the Bible tells us.

Our Lord Jesus, God's Son, died so we could be forgiven for our sins and be God's children. That's more than fair, isn't it?

- Since God is always fair, how does God want us to treat other people?

▼ ▼ ▼

Bible Verse
God plays no favorites. Acts 10:34 (HBC)

For Older Children
In 2 Samuel 12:1-6 there is a story about two men, one rich and one poor. What did the rich man do that wasn't fair?

Let's Pray
Lord Jesus, You are always more than fair to everybody. Make me more like You.

What About Rules?

Some children like rules; many do not. Jessica didn't like to obey rules. She liked to jump on the bed, run in the house, and tease her little sister even though she knew it was against the rules.

- What are some of the rules at your house?
- What are some of the rules at school?
- What would happen if there were no rules?
- What would you do if you could do anything you wanted to do?
- Why would that not be good?

God gave His children some rules to follow. We call them the Ten Commandments.

- What are some of God's commandments?
- Why did God give His children these rules?

Sometimes we don't like to follow the rules—even if they are good for us. So how can we enjoy rules, especially if they are *God's* rules?

The Bible says Jesus frees us from rules. That doesn't mean we can do anything we please. It means He makes us *want* to do what God wants us to do, and then we don't obey God's rules just because we *have* to.

- How does loving God make it easier to obey His rules?
- Are there any rules at your house?
- What are they?

When we love God, we don't obey His rules because we *have* to. We obey them because we *want* to. That makes God's rules easy to follow. Isn't it nice to have a loving God who wants us to feel free and happy?

▼ ▼ ▼

Bible Verse
Freedom is what we have. Christ has set us free! Galatians 5:1 (TEV)

For Older Children
Make a list of rules you don't like but are willing to obey because Jesus wants you to do so.

Let's Pray
Dear Jesus, I'm glad You don't *force* me to do what God wants me to do. Your love makes me want to obey God willingly.

Choosing the Best

In a story about a girl named Lili, a puppet said to her, "If you could have anything you wanted, what would you ask for?" At first Lili answered, "I don't know." But then she said, "I would ask for someone to love me."

- What would *you* choose if you could have anything *you* wanted?

Jesus once told a story about a man who was searching for beautiful pearls. Pearls are a beautiful, expensive jewel that some women wear. They're found in oysters. When the man found a very beautiful and valuable pearl, he sold all the pearls he had so he could buy the very special pearl he had found. He wanted the best pearl more than anything else.

Life with God is like the best pearl you could ever find or buy. It's more beautiful and more valuable than anything else you have. It's worth giving up whatever you have in order to have that life with God.

- What are some of the things you would be willing to give up in order to live with Jesus?
- Is there anything you would choose rather than Jesus?

Jesus is like that best pearl. He's someone who will always love you and be good to you. He's worth more than anything else you could ever choose to have.

▼ ▼ ▼

Bible Verse
The kingdom of heaven is like ... fine pearls. Matthew 13:45 (TEV)

For Older Children
You can read more about the man and his pearl in Matthew 13:45-46.

Let's Pray
Dear Jesus, You are worth more than anything else I could have. Please help me to love You above anything else.

If You Were a King or Queen

Have you ever played a game called "King of the Hill"? The person at the top of the hill or a high place tries to keep the others from getting to the top. Sometimes it can be a very rough game if people push and shove too much. The person on top wants to keep being the king or queen.

There are very few real kings and queens left in the world. Some of the ones we know, like the Queen of England or the King of Sweden, don't really rule their country the way kings and queens used to. Kings and queens used to make all the laws for their countries, and everyone had to obey them. Kings and queens today have other people make the laws, but they still have some power.

- If you were king or queen and could decide what would happen in your country, what would you do for the people?
- What kinds of laws would you make?
- What would you do for the children?

Jesus was called a king. He is king of the whole world and rules with His love. But when He lived on earth, not everybody wanted Him to be their king. Some of the people hung Him on a cross to die. Jesus let them kill Him and became alive again so that His people could live forever with God.

- What kind of king is Jesus?
- How does Jesus rule His people?

▼ ▼ ▼

Bible Verse
He [Jesus] is Lord of lords and King of kings. Revelation 17:14 (TEV)

For Older Children
You can read about Jesus' crown of thorns in Matthew 27:27-31. Remember that He let this happen to Him because He loves us.

Let's Pray
Lord Jesus, my King, You showed how much You loved me when You died for me. Rule me and all people with Your love.

When It's Dark Outside

Some people like to sit in the dark, but most people like to be where it's light and bright.

- What do you like best—a dark night or a bright sunny day?

When it's stormy and rainy, it's often dark even in the daytime and especially at night. No sun or no moon and stars can be seen in the sky. When the roads are wet, even the lights from cars can't be seen very well.

- Why would it be foolish to go anywhere in the dark without a light?
- What would happen if people drove cars in the dark without their lights on?

The Bible says God's Word is like a lamp for our feet and a light for our path.

- What does the Bible help us to see?
- How can you use the Bible to light your path?

The Bible is a light that helps us to see the greatest light in the world. This light is a person. Jesus is the light of the world. What does He help us to see?

Without knowing Jesus, people live in darkness. What happens when people walk around in the dark? Just close your eyes and try to walk in the dark. But if your eyes are open and you can see Jesus, His light will show you God and where to go and what to do. His light makes your whole life bright and safe and happy.

▼ ▼ ▼

Bible Verse
Your word is a lamp to guide me and a light for my path. Psalm 119:105 (TEV)

For Older Children
In John 8:12 Jesus says He is the light of the world. Look up the verse in your Bible to see what He promises you there.

Let's Pray
Lord God, thank You for the Bible. Help me to see that Jesus is the light I need to follow in order to live with You.

Going to Church

Bobby's family always went to church on Sundays, even when they were on vacation. Have you ever gone to church when you were on a trip? How was it different from your church at home? How was it the same?

In a poem in the Bible a man says, "I was glad when they said to me, 'Let us go to the house of the Lord.'"

- What was the house of the Lord Jesus or the house of the Lord God?
- Why was the man glad when someone said to him, "Let's go to church"?
- What do you like about going to church?

Some people live in countries where it's against the law to go to church. They have to meet in secret. Other people are too sick to go to church. Isn't it nice to be healthy and to live in a country where you can go to church?

The next time you're at church, think about all the things you like about going to church. Then say what the man in the Bible said, and thank God for your church.

▼ ▼ ▼

Bible Verse
I was glad when they said to me, "Let us go to the LORD's house." Psalm 122:1 (TEV)

For Older Children
In Luke 2:41-49 you can read the story of how Jesus once went to the church in Jerusalem without His parents.

Let's Pray
Lord God, make me glad when anyone says to me, "Let's go to church."

Love Is . . .

Teachers sometimes start a sentence and ask their students to finish it. What kind of endings could you put to the words "Love is . . ."?

Doctors say babies need TLC. That means *tender loving care*. How could you give TLC to a baby? How could you give TLC to an older person?

- In what other ways do people show love to others?
- If you refused to talk with me, what would that show?

People love also by helping others or by giving someone a present or by saying something nice to a person.

- What could you say to me that would be nice?
- What do people say by giving someone flowers or candy?

The Bible says God is love and loves us. This means that everything God does is good and everything He wants for us is good.

- How did Jesus show us that God loves us?
- What did Jesus do for us?

The Bible says Jesus died for us on a cross. That's the very most anyone could do.

- What are some things God does for you every day?
- How will you show love to someone this week?

▼ ▼ ▼

Bible Verse
God so loved the world that he gave his only son. John 3:16
(HBC)

For Older Children
You can read more about God's love in 1 John 4:7-12.

Let's Pray
Dear God, people love You because You loved them first. Don't ever let me forget how much You love me. Make me a person who loves others.

How You Can Be a Star

"Twinkle, twinkle, little star; how I wonder what you are," sang a little girl as she looked up into the sky one night. Then she tried to count the stars. But she soon gave up.

The Bible says God made the stars. There are so many that no one could ever count them. The stars twinkle to tell us how wonderful God is.

When Jesus was born, God put a brand new star in the sky. It told some wise men in a faraway country that someone very special had been born on earth. Somehow those men knew that the baby was God's Son.

Do you know the story of the wise men? They came to a city called Bethlehem to worship the baby Jesus. They followed the new star, and it showed them where Jesus was staying with His parents, Mary and Joseph.

Because Jesus' birthday is remembered at Christmas, people use stars for Christmas decorations. Most stars have five points, but there's a special Christmas star that has many points—at least twenty. It points in every direction and is called a *Moravian star*. What do you think it says about Jesus?

Some people are called stars when they do something special. You can do something special by helping people find Jesus. Then you'll be a *Christmas* star!

- What are some things you will do if you're a Christmas star?
- How can you help people find Jesus?

▼ ▼ ▼

Bible Verse
Men who studied the stars came . . . to Jerusalem and asked, "Where is the baby born to be the king of the Jews?" Matthew 2:1-2 (TEV)

For Older Children
In Matthew 2:1-12 you can read more about the Christmas star that led the wise men to Jesus.

Let's Pray
Lord God, make me a star that will lead people to Jesus.

Being a Christian

You've probably heard that some people are called *Christians*. Not everybody is a Christian. Christians are people who listen to Jesus and obey His teachings.

- Do you know anyone who is a Christian?
- Are you a Christian?

Being a Christian is kind of like being one of Jesus' lambs

or sheep. He called Himself our shepherd because He takes care of His people like a good shepherd takes care of his sheep.

Jesus protects us from danger like a shepherd protects his sheep from wolves. If wolves attack the sheep, the shepherd stands up and fights the wolves to save his sheep.

Jesus also said, "My sheep listen to my voice . . . and they follow me." Sheep follow their shepherd because they recognize his voice. They won't follow someone whose voice they don't know.

- How do Christians follow Jesus?
- How can you listen to Jesus and obey His voice?
- What are some things Jesus has told you to do?
- Where can you hear and learn Jesus' teachings?

▼ ▼ ▼

Bible Verse
Jesus said, "My sheep listen to my voice . . . and they follow me." John 10:27 (TEV)

For Older Children
In John 10:11-15 you can read more about Jesus being our Good Shepherd. In verse 28, see what Jesus said He gives to His sheep.

Let's Pray
Lord Jesus, my Good Shepherd, help me to listen to Your voice and follow You.

Knowing Jesus

When Jesus was born in Bethlehem, an angel told some shepherds, "On this day the Savior, Christ the Lord, was born." Do you know why Jesus is called "the Lord"? And do you know why Jesus was called "the Savior"? Because He came to save people like us from our sins.

- What do you know about Jesus?
- What kind of person do you think Jesus was?

When Jesus was alive on earth He told His disciples, "Whoever has seen me has seen my Father." By Father, Jesus meant God. He was telling the disciples that He was God. Jesus and God are exactly alike.

- What can you know about God by knowing Jesus?

Some people say twins are alike, but they are never exactly alike. They may look pretty much alike, but they are different people in lots of ways.

But when Jesus said, "The Father and I are one" He meant, "God, our Father in heaven, and I are the same in every way. We are exactly alike."

- In what ways are Jesus and God alike?

▼ ▼ ▼

Bible Verse
Jesus said, "Whoever has seen me has seen the Father." John 14:9 (TEV)

For Older Children
In John 14:8-11 you can read more about Jesus being exactly the same as God.

Let's Pray
Jesus, I'm glad You've shown me what God is like, because You are a very loving person.

Making Music

There are many different ways to make music. Can you name some of them?

- Can you sing, whistle, or hum?
- Can you play the piano, a trumpet, a flute, or some other instrument?
- How does hearing music usually make you feel?

People who write music for other people to play or sing are called *composers*. There have been many composers who have written music that other people play. Can you name some? Maybe someday you'll be able to be a composer of music.

There are many different kinds of music.

- Can you name some kinds of music people play or listen to?
- What kind of music do you like best?

Mary Beth loved to play the piano. Sometimes she would sing the songs as she played them God's children have lots of reasons for making music. What are some? What do you think is the *best* reason?

The Bible says everything alive should sing God's praises. The people who know Jesus have the most reasons to praise God. Do you know why?

- How do people who love God make music in their church services?
- How can you join them in making music?

▼ ▼ ▼

Bible Verse
Praise the LORD, all living creatures! Psalm 150:6 (TEV)

For Older Children
Psalm 150 talks about some of the ways you can make music to praise God. Look it up in your Bible.

Let's Pray
Dear Jesus, Your love makes me want to praise God with music and singing.

Why Pray?

A lot of people pray. Prayer is talking to God. Some people think they have to kneel to pray. Others stand and fold their hands and bow their heads. Some like to walk when they pray.

- Why do people talk to God?
- Why doesn't God care whether we're kneeling or standing when we pray?
- What's important to God?
- How do you usually pray?
- Why is God always glad to have you pray to Him?

Once there was a girl who prayed for her mother every day for more than a year. She asked God to take away her mother's sickness. But her mother died anyway.

- Why do you think God didn't heal her mother?
- What good did it do to pray to God?
- Why does the Bible tell us never to give up praying?

Sometimes God doesn't answer our prayers the way we want Him to. Sometimes He says yes to the things we ask Him and sometimes He says no. At other times He doesn't answer our prayers right away, but makes us wait before He answers. He always has good reasons. No matter what, we can always be sure God loves us. He does the very best for us.

▼ ▼ ▼

Bible Verse
Always be happy, never stop praying, and be thankful no matter what happens. 1 Thessalonians 5:16-18 (HBC)

For Older Children
In Romans 8:28 God gives us a wonderful promise. You'll want to memorize it so you can always remember it.

Let's Pray
Lord God, I know You love me even when my prayers aren't answered right away or when You say no. Help me to keep on praying and to be thankful for Your love no matter what happens.

What We All Can't Do
There's a book called *I Can't Make a Flower*.

- What kind of flowers *can't* you make?
- Who can make real flowers?
- How does God make real flowers?

There's a song that says, "Only God can make a tree." Can you think of anything else that only God can do?

- Could you make a dog or a cat or a fish or a bird?
- What else can't people do?

The Bible says that a long time ago God made all the plants and animals in the world. He also planned a way for these things to make themselves.

- Do you know how new plants are made?
- How about new animals?

Aren't you glad God helped your parents make you and that God continues to keep you alive? God has lots of good plans for you.

▼ ▼ ▼

Bible Verse
In the beginning . . . God said, "Let every kind of . . . plant start to grow on the earth and fruit trees with their seeds inside the fruit." Genesis 1:11 (HBC)

For Older Children
You can read in Genesis 1:20-25 how God made the plants and animals.

Let's Pray
Dear God, everything You do is wonderful and good. I'm glad You helped my parents make me and that You keep me alive.

Grapevines and Branches

Have you ever seen grapes grow? They grow on branches that are connected to a vine. The vine goes into the ground and brings water and other food to the branches so they can make plump, juicy grapes. If the branch is cut off from the vine, it can't grow any grapes.

- Do you like grapes?
- What kind do you like best, the green ones or the purple ones?

Jesus once said that He was like a vine on which grapes grow. The branches are His friends and disciples. They are the people who love Him. The grapes are the good things they do.

- Are you growing grapes?
- What are some good things you can do for others?

Jesus said that any branch that doesn't grow grapes is thrown away. It's useless. Jesus wants us to grow grapes by doing loving things for other people. But to do that, we have to stay connected to Jesus.

- How can you stay connected to Jesus and have Jesus live in you?
- In what ways does Jesus come to you?

▼ ▼ ▼

Bible Verse
Jesus said: "I am the vine and you are the branches. Get your life from me and you will bear much fruit." John 15:5 (HBC)

For Older Children
You can read more about the vine and branches Jesus talked about in John 15:1-17.

Let's Pray
Lord Jesus, keep me close to you and live in me so I'll be like a branch of sweet grapes.

Why Be Sad?

Grownup people get sad sometimes. They get sad when someone they love is sick or when they hurt. They get sad when they feel scared or alone. Do children get sad too?

- What makes you sad?

In the Bible a man named Isaiah wrote, "Haven't you heard? Haven't you been told that God sits above the earth and rules everything? And that His power is very great? He never gets tired or goes to sleep (Isaiah 40:28)."

Because God is in charge, Isaiah said you can trust God to take away your sadness. When God takes away your sadness, He makes you feel like you can fly like an eagle or run forever and not get tired.

- Have you ever seen an eagle fly?
- What do eagles or other big birds do?
- How would you feel if you could fly like an eagle?
- What happens when you run and run?
- What would it be like to be able to run and never get tired?

Isaiah also said, "Why be sad? Why complain? God sees

what is happening to you. He knows what your trouble is. And God will help you if you want Him to."

- So what can you do the next time you feel sad?
- How can you help other people who feel sad?

▼ ▼ ▼

Bible Verse
Those who trust in the LORD for help . . . will rise on wings like eagles. Isaiah 40:31 (TEV)

For Older Children
Draw a picture of a bird flying high in the sky. Think of yourself as being the bird.

Let's Pray
Dear God, when I'm sad, remind me to wait for You to do things for me. Then make me feel like an eagle flying high in the sky.

Let's Talk About God
Do you ever think about God and what He's like? When you love someone you want to know about that person, and you like to talk about him or her too.

- What can you tell about God?
- What's God like?
- Where is God?

Jesus called God His Father in heaven. If you are one of God's children, He is your Father too. Jesus told us to call God our Father when we pray to Him.

■ In what ways is God like a good father?

God was in the person Jesus, and He lives in the people who love Jesus. Jesus said that He and His Father come to the people who love Him. God lives in them and is always with them.

God gave His children rules for how they should live. The first of God's rules called commandments is, "You must have no other gods besides me." A god is a person or a thing you love the most.

■ What are some of the things people love more than God?

■ What will you do if you love God more than anything else?

▼ ▼ ▼

Bible Verse
You must have no other gods besides me. Exodus 20:3 (HBC)

For Older Children
In Exodus 20:4-17 you can read more of the rules God gave His children.

Let's Pray
Lord God, there is no god as great and good as You. Help me to love You more than anything else.

Your Sunday School

Do you go to Sunday school? Sunday schools teach about God. Children learn Bible stories and songs when they go to Sunday school.

- What happens in your Sunday school?
- Why is it important to attend Sunday school regularly?
- If you were a Sunday school teacher, what would you do with your class?

Jesus went to a synagogue school when He was a boy. He learned the stories about God in the first part of the Bible. It's called the Old Testament. Do you know any of those stories? Jesus also learned poems called *psalms*.

When Jesus was a boy He loved going to His church. One time when Jesus' family was on a trip, Jesus went to the temple church and stayed so long that His parents started to travel home without Him! When they went back, they looked all over the big city for Him. They finally found Him sitting with some teachers in the temple. He was learning about His Father in heaven.

- What does that teach you to do?
- What have you learned by going to Sunday school?

▼ ▼ ▼

Bible Verse
[When Jesus was twelve] his parents found Jesus in the temple. He was sitting with the teachers, listening to them and asking them questions. Luke 2:46 (HBC)

For Older Children
You can read about Jesus and the temple in Luke 2:41-51.

Let's Pray
Lord Jesus, when You were a child, You knew the importance of learning God's Word. Make me regular in my Sunday school

and church attendance, so I'll grow up knowing You and my Father in heaven.

Names of God

Most people have at least two names. Your first name is called your Christian name. How did you get your last name? Some people also have at least one or two middle names. Do you know your middle name?

Someone once said, "A rose by any other name would smell as sweet."

- Would a rose still be a sweet-smelling flower if it were called something else?
- Would you be the same person you are if you had a different name?

God has many names. In the Bible God is called by more than one hundred different names.

- What do you call God?
- What are some other names people use in talking about God?

The Bible also says there is one name that is above every other name. It stands out. It is more important than any other name because it's the name of the most important person who ever lived on earth.

- Do you know who that person is?
- Do you know why He's so important?

There's a hymn that says,

> Jesus, my Shepherd, Guardian, Friend,
> My Prophet, Priest, and King,
> My Lord, my Life, my Way, my End,
> Accept the praise I bring.

- What names does the hymn give to Jesus?
- How do many people honor the name of Jesus?

▼ ▼ ▼

Bible Verse
God highly honored Jesus and gave him a name that is greater than any other name. Philippians 2:9 (HBC)

For Older Children
Look in a hymnal if you can and try to find at least six names of Jesus.

Let's Pray
Dear Jesus, You have a wonderful name. Keep me from ever saying it without a good reason.

Where Is Heaven?

Did you ever hear someone say "Thank heaven" because something bad didn't happen or because something good happened? There's even a song that says, "Thank heaven for little girls."

- What do you thank heaven for?

Heaven is where God is, so saying "thank heaven" is a way of saying "thank God." Jesus is in heaven too.

Some people think heaven is way up high in the sky. What do you think?

- If heaven is where God is, and God is everywhere, where must heaven be?

Thinking about heaven can be a little confusing! But wherever heaven is, we know that if we belong to Jesus we'll always be with God.

So ask Jesus to keep you close to Him every day. Then you'll be with Him in heaven. You'll also be very happy.

- What do you think it's like to be in heaven?

Whenever you hear someone talk about heaven, be sure to thank Jesus that He's there and wants you to be with Him.

▼ ▼ ▼

Bible Verse
Jesus Christ . . . has gone into heaven and is . . . ruling. 1 Peter 3:22 (TEV)

For Older Children
In Luke 24:50-53 you can read how Jesus went to heaven after He died and became alive again.

Let's Pray
Dear Jesus, keep me with You every day, so I'll always be with You in heaven.

What About Angels?

Have you ever seen an angel? Angels are spirits. They don't have bodies of their own, but they can live in any kind of body.

Usually angels are pictured as people with wings who can fly. But they really don't have wings. The wings on angels in pictures tell us that angels can move fast from one place to another.

Angels are God's helpers. They bring people messages from God, and they are sent by God to help people. Sometimes angels look like people.

There are many stories about angels in the Bible. Angels told Abraham and Sarah that they would have a baby. An angel also told Mary that she would be Jesus' mother. Lots of angels told the shepherds in the fields outside of Bethlehem about the baby Jesus.

Once when some men were put in prison for being friends of Jesus, God sent an angel to open the prison doors and let them out. An angel at Jesus' grave told some women that He was alive again.

- Can you think of any other angel stories in the Bible?
- What's your favorite story about angels?

The Bible says God will put His angels in charge of taking care of us if we are one of His children. If you'll remember that, how will you feel?

▼ ▼ ▼

Bible Verse
God will put his angels in charge of you, to guard you wherever you go. Psalm 91:11 (HBC)

For Older Children
Make a drawing of how you picture an angel. Put your picture in your room where you can see it.

Let's Pray
Lord God, thank You for angels. Please put one of Your angels in charge of taking care of me, so I'll be safe from dangers that could hurt me.

LET'S TALK ABOUT SPECIAL DAYS

What Do You Like About Christmas?

Do you like Christmas? Most people do. It's a time when families get together and people are kind to each other.

- What do you like about Christmas?
- Why are decorations exciting?

Friends of Jesus have a very special reason for enjoying Christmas. Do you know what it is? A bumper sticker on a car asked, "Whose birthday is Christmas anyway?" You know the answer: It's Jesus' birthday. But do you know *why* the question is asked? It's because many people forget that Christmas is the celebration of Jesus' birthday.

When it's your birthday, you get presents. On Jesus' birthday, you get presents too. Maybe the presents we get show us how good God was in giving us Jesus. He makes people love and give presents to each other.

- Have you ever given Jesus a birthday present?

There are lots of things to remind us that Christmas is Jesus' birthday.

- How do the Christmas lights remind you of Jesus?
- Have you ever seen a poinsettia? It's a plant with red flowers that people have at Christmas. How does it remind you of Jesus?

Maybe you've heard the saying that "Jesus is the reason for the season." Without Jesus there wouldn't be Christmas. How can you celebrate Jesus' birthday this Christmas?

▼ ▼ ▼

Bible Verse
This very day, in King David's town, the Savior, Christ the Lord, was born. Luke 2:11 (HBC)

For Older Children
You can read about the first Christmas presents in Matthew 2:1-11.

Let's Pray
Happy birthday, Jesus. Thank You for coming to earth to give me life with God.

Easter Eggs and Rabbits

Some people hang plastic eggs on trees outside their house at Easter. Others decorate real eggs and have an Easter egg hunt.

- Have you ever been to an Easter egg hunt?
- What do the eggs tell us about Easter?

At some Easter parties there's an Easter bunny. He's called Peter Rabbit or Peter Cottontail. What does he do? Some children receive chocolate rabbits or little candy chickens in a basket on Easter morning.

- What do the rabbits and chicks tell us about Easter?

At Easter baby animals and birds appear, and there is new life in the trees and flowers that begin to blossom. But all these wonderful sights in spring don't tell us the *best* Easter news of all. Do you know what that is?

Easter tells us that Jesus, our God, is alive. He gives a new kind of life to people. He makes children happy children of God.

- Do you know how Jesus does that?

Jesus also promises to give people a life with God in heaven when they die. Isn't that exciting? So, if you like hunting, hurry and hunt for Jesus. He's everywhere, and He's worth finding— more than eggs or candy or anything else.

▼ ▼ ▼

Bible Verse
Jesus said, "I am the living one! I was dead, but now I am alive forever and ever." Revelation 1:18 (TEV)

For Older Children
You can read the story about the first Easter day in Matthew 28:1-10.

Let's Pray
Happy Easter, Jesus. Thank You for making things alive and for promising to give me life with God in heaven.

LET'S TALK ABOUT PEOPLE

What Do You Eat?

Most children like hamburgers and French fries. What's your favorite food? Think of the last time your parents took you to a restaurant. What did you order? What do you usually eat for breakfast?

- Did you know that your body stays healthy only if it gets the right kinds of food?
- What are some of the better foods to eat? How about fruits and vegetables?

People who study foods say we need to eat fruits and vegetables every day. What kinds of fruit do you like? What kinds of vegetables?

Doctors tell us that fish and seafood are better for our bodies than fatty sausage. Too much fat in your body keeps your blood from going to your heart. That's what often gives people heart attacks.

- What will happen to your body if you eat a lot of candy?
- Why is soda pop not good for you?
- Why is milk better?

The Bible tells about a young man named Daniel. He was chosen by a king to become a leader in the king's country. While learning what he needed to know, Daniel lived in the king's palace. The food at the palace was rich and always served with lots of wine.

But Daniel decided he wouldn't eat and drink what would harm his body. So he asked his guard to let him and his friends eat vegetables and drink water for ten days. After ten days

Daniel and his three friends looked healthier and stronger than the men who ate the king's food.

Remember, to have a healthy body, don't eat a lot of sugar and fatty foods. Fruits and vegetables are better for you.

▼ ▼ ▼

Bible Verse
Daniel decided he wouldn't eat the king's rich food or drink the wine. Daniel 1:8 (HBC)

For Older Children
You can read more about the story of Daniel in Daniel 1.

Let's Pray
Lord God, I want my body to be healthy and strong, so make me careful about what I eat and drink.

Why Giving Is Better Than Receiving

Most people like to get presents. On birthdays and at Christmas and at any other time, children can hardly wait to open their packages.

- Why do you like getting presents?
- What's the best present you ever received?

It's fun to wonder what you're getting. It's nice to know you're being loved. But here's a surprise. It's even more fun to *give* presents. Jesus said, "There is more happiness in giving than in receiving (Acts 20:35)."

Loretta was a busy mother of two young children, but she took time to bake and make soup and other food for people who were old and alone or sick. Doing this and bringing food

to people made her happy. What she did made those who received her gifts happy too.

- Do you remember a time when you made someone happy by giving something to them?
- How did giving make you feel?

Do you know who gives people the most? God gave us His Son Jesus to be our Savior. And Jesus gave us His life so we could have God's love. God likes to receive our love and gifts, but He gives us much more than we could ever give Him.

▼ ▼ ▼

Bible Verse
There is more happiness in giving than in receiving. Acts 20:35 (TEV)

For Older Children
You can read about a woman who gave God everything she had in Mark 12:41-44.

Let's Pray
Dear Jesus, You gave Your life for me. Make me glad to give gifts to You and to others.

Your Teachers
Teachers are very important people. Good teachers are blessings from God. They not only teach subjects like math and reading; they also teach students how to grow up to be good people.

- Who is your favorite teacher? Why?
- What is your teacher good at teaching?

- Would you like to become a teacher when you grow up?
- What do you think makes a good teacher?
- What's the best thing a teacher ever did for you?

There are many different kinds of teachers. There are piano teachers, soccer coaches, Sunday school teachers, and camp leaders.

- What other kinds of teachers can you think of?

Jesus was called a teacher. He was the greatest teacher who ever lived.

- What kinds of things did Jesus teach?
- What have you learned from Jesus?
- How does Jesus still teach many, many people today?

Here's some good news: Jesus wants all of us to be teachers. He said, "Teach others to do what I have taught you."

- What has Jesus taught you?
- How can you be a teacher for Jesus?

You can be a teacher by what you say and do. Try teaching others God's love this week.

▼ ▼ ▼

Bible Verse
Jesus said, "Teach them to do everything I have commanded."
Matthew 28:20 (HBC)

For Older Children
Some of Jesus' most famous teachings are in His Sermon on the

Mount. You can read part of the Sermon on the Mount in Matthew 5:3-11.

Let's Pray
Dear Jesus, I'm glad I'm being taught by You. Help me to teach others about You.

Keeping a Secret

Mary Jane asked her friend Julie not to tell anyone she really liked a boy named Peter. He lived near her and rode the same school bus. But Mary Jane tried not to look at Peter or talk to him at the bus stop. She didn't want Peter to know she liked him.

Julie thought it would be fun to tell others what Mary Jane had told her. She whispered the secret to others on the bus and giggled about it.

- Why do people like to tell secrets?
- Why is it so hard to keep a secret?

Telling secrets can sometimes do a lot of harm. How did Julie hurt her friend by telling her secret? How did she hurt her friendship with Mary Jane?

The Bible says a tattletale tells secrets, but a person who is a good friend keeps a secret. God wants you to keep other people's secrets to yourself, but you can tell God or your parents *your* secrets. Why can you do that?

▼ ▼ ▼

Bible Verse
A gossip goes about telling secrets, but one who is trustworthy in spirit keeps [the secret]. Proverbs 11:13 (NRSV)

For Older Children
In Matthew 6:6 Jesus tells you something to do in secret. What is it?

Let's Pray
Lord God, help me to keep people's secrets and not be a tattletale.

Talking to Grandma and Grandpa

Talking to someone is one of the ways we show love. People who love each other like to talk to each other.

Talking is a good way to love an older person. Older people are often lonesome and like to have children talk to them. Grandparents especially like talking with their grandchildren. When their grandchildren talk to them, it makes them very happy.

■ When was the last time you talked to your grandparents?

- What did you talk about?
- Have you ever asked them what they did when they were children? Or what their school was like? Or what kind of work they did when they were young?

Maybe they still have pictures of when they were children. You'll be surprised how different they looked when they were younger. If they don't live near you, you can call them on the telephone or send them a letter. You don't have to wait for a special reason, like a birthday, to talk to them. Surprise them by talking to them just because you love them.

What would be some other things you could ask them about? They'll be glad to tell you if they went to Sunday school and what they learned about God when they were younger. That will help you get to know them better.

▼ ▼ ▼

Bible Verse
Young men and women alike, old and young together! Let them praise the name of the LORD! Psalm 148:12-13 (NRSV)

For Older Children
Leviticus 19:32 tells you how to respect older people like your grandparents. You may want to read the verse in your Bible.

Let's Pray
Lord God, You tell us in the Bible to respect the elderly. Help me to respect my grandparents and remember that talking to my grandparents is a way to love them.

Cruel Children

Do you know any cruel children? Cruel people like to hurt others. They enjoy seeing people suffer. Sometimes they enjoy hurting animals too.

Billy was a cruel boy. He teased other boys and girls to make them cry. He hit other children. He even pulled his dog's tail just to be mean.

Children can be cruel in what they say and do. Often at school they make fun of someone they don't like. Or they won't talk to a child who is different.

- Do you remember a time when children were cruel to you or someone you know?
- Can you imagine Jesus ever being cruel? Why not?

Our God is a loving God and wants us to be kind and loving too. Kind people feel badly about the cruel things people do to others. They try not to be cruel.

- What can you do when you see someone hurting another person?
- What will help you not to be cruel?
- How can you be kind to others?

Being cruel to others is a terrible sin. Be glad that God forgives us when we are sorry we have hurt others. God's love helps us not to be cruel.

▼ ▼ ▼

Bible Verse
The LORD is pleased with good people. Proverbs 12:2 (TEV)

For Older Children
You can read in Genesis 16 how Sarah was cruel to her maid Hagar.

Let's Pray
Lord God, help me to be good to others. Please forgive me whenever I'm cruel.

Loving Children Who Are Different

Michelle learned in Sunday school that God loves the people of every country and every color of skin. She knew that Jesus died for them all and plays no favorites. So she enjoyed being with children who looked different. She thought they were more interesting than children like herself.

But not everyone loves people who are different.

- Why do children often make fun of a person who is different?
- What kind of children at school seem different?
- Why are children who are different sometimes not liked?

Older people sometimes say things about people they don't like. The next time you hear that, ask them why they don't like the people they talk about. Maybe they'll start to wonder about that.

In the Bible, God told us to love everybody. God doesn't look at what people look like. He looks at their hearts. If God loves people who are different, why can't we?

- Why does God make people different from each other?
- What will help you love children who are different?

▼ ▼ ▼

Bible Verse
The LORD is good to all. Psalm 145:9 (NRSV)

For Older Children
In Galations 3:26-28 the apostle Paul says God sees us all as being the same. You may want to read the passage in your Bible.

Let's Pray
Lord God, I'm glad You made each one of us different and You love us all. Help me to enjoy and love people who are different.

People Who Get Angry

Jimmy wanted to go swimming at his friend's house. His mother said he had to take his dog for a walk first. Jimmy didn't want to take his dog for a walk and became very angry.

- What are some reasons people get angry?
- What makes you angry?
- What do you do when you get angry?

Jesus got angry. But He didn't get angry when He didn't get His own way. He didn't get angry even when people hung Him on a cross. Jesus got angry when He saw people doing something wrong.

Children sometimes do wrong things. They tell lies. They break other people's property. They say mean things. They scribble on buildings. They steal things that don't belong to them. They fight with each other.

- What are some of the things you do that are wrong?

■ Why do you think those things might make Jesus angry?

Jesus never hurt anyone when He got angry. Instead of hurting people, He taught them to love and forgive. When you feel yourself getting angry, stop and ask yourself what Jesus would do.

▼ ▼ ▼

Bible Verse
Let everyone be quick to listen, slow to speak, slow to anger. James 1:19 (NRSV)

For Older Children
In 1 Peter 2:21-23 you can read about the example Jesus gave us to follow.

Let's Pray
Dear Jesus, when I feel myself getting angry, help me to stop and think about how You would act.

The Man Who Said "Thank You"

Once when Jesus was walking along a road, He met ten men who had leprosy. Leprosy is a very bad skin sickness. When the ten men saw Jesus, they asked Him to heal them and make their leprosy go away.

Jesus told the men to go to their church. As the men were walking to the church, their leprosy went away. Nine of the men kept going. But the tenth man was so happy to be healed that he ran back to Jesus and thanked Jesus for making him well.

Jesus was happy that the one man came back to say "thank

you." But He was sad that the other nine men who were healed didn't come back to thank Him. He asked, "Where are the other nine?"

The Bible often tells us to be thankful, to thank God for all good things and to thank people when they do good things for us.

- Have you ever done something nice for someone? How would you feel if that person didn't say thank you?
- What are some of the things God has done for you?
- Have you thanked God for those things?

When people do nice things for you, try to remember to thank them too. You'll see how happy that will make them.

▼ ▼ ▼

Bible Verse
Always give thanks for everything to God the Father. Ephesians 5:20 (TEV)

For Older Children
You can read more about the man who thanked Jesus in Luke 17:11-19.

Let's Pray
Dear God, You are the one who makes all good things happen. Let me never forget to thank You and those who do good for You.

Is Honesty the Best Policy?
A young man bought a suit for a wedding and returned it after the wedding. He told the store he didn't like it. A mother bought toys for her children. After they played with them for a few days

she returned them. She said they weren't what her children wanted.

Was there anything wrong in what these people did? Some people say that "honesty is the best policy." That means it's always better to tell the truth than to lie. Is that so?

- Why is it better to tell the truth than to lie?
- Who always knows whether we're telling the truth?
- What happens when we lie instead of telling the truth?

The Bible says God wants people to tell each other the truth. He doesn't like it when we lie. Imagine what it would be like if everybody lied all the time. How would you know what was true?

Jesus always spoke the truth and never lied. He said that everything He taught was the truth. Why is that a good thing to know?

- What can you do when someone catches you telling a lie?
- How can you be sure that Jesus will forgive you when you lie?

▼ ▼ ▼

Bible Verse
Everyone ought to speak the truth. Ephesians 4:25 (HBC)

For Older Children
In Genesis 20:1-14 there is a story about a time Abraham lied and what happened. Find it and read it. Then tell someone what you read.

Let's Pray
Dear Jesus, I know You want me to speak the truth and not lie. Please help me to be honest.

Children Singing

Matt likes to sing to himself while he walks his dog or works on a project. It makes him feel good, especially when he's sad.

- Why do most children like to sing?
- What's your favorite song?
- How does singing make you feel?

Sometimes singing in a group is even more fun than singing alone. A big group of people who sing together is called a *choir*. Did you ever notice that people smile when they see children singing together? Why is that?

The Bible says all of God's children should sing to the Lord. The Lord is another name for God. People who know God like to sing about Him and to Him. They thank and praise Him with their songs.

- Why do people sing praises to God?
- For what can you thank or praise God?

The Bible also says everything in the world sings God's praises. Even trees sing God's praises.

- What do you think the trees say about God?
- What about the clouds in the sky? What do they say?
- How about the birds? What do they say with their songs?

There's a hymn that says, "Athlete and band; loud cheering people. Sing to the Lord a new song! Daughter and son; loud praying members! Sing to the Lord a new song!" Can you think of a new song to sing to God? Let's try to make a song.

▼ ▼ ▼

Bible Verse
Worship the Lord gladly and come to him with singing. Psalm 100:2 (HBC)

For Older Children
Could you write a poem that praises God?

Let's Pray
Lord God, everything You do makes me want to sing Your praises.

When People Play

A lot of animals like to play. It's fun to watch them and play with them too.

- How do cats play?
- How do dogs play?
- What other animals are fun to watch when they play?

The zoo is a good place to watch animals play. Young lions like to play by fighting each other. They snarl and jump at each other, but they never bite when they're playing. Monkeys like to jump from one tree to another or on top of another monkey and then run away. Young bears like to wrestle. A lot of other young

animals like to chase each other. Some animals just like to run and jump in the air.

Most children like to play too. It's important to play and have fun. Children who don't play often grow up sad. Children who play a lot become happier.

- What do you enjoy doing when you feel playful?
- What do you and your friends like to do when you play together?
- How do your parents play with you?

The Bible tells us that once King David was so happy with God that he danced. Have you ever been so happy that you danced?

- What do you do when you're happy?

Jesus probably played games when He was a boy. What kinds of games do you think He played?

▼ ▼ ▼

Bible Verse
David danced with all his might before the Lord [because he was happy]. 2 Samuel 6:5 (HBC)

For Older Children
Make a list of games children play. Circle the ones you like best.

Let's Pray
Dear Jesus, Your love makes people so happy, they want to dance and play. Make me that happy too.

The Fun of Giving

Christmas is a happy time. One of the reasons is the fun people have in shopping for gifts, wrapping them, and giving them to people they love. Giving makes the givers happy.

Topper was a dog who liked to give gifts to his owner. Every morning he would sit at the bottom of the steps in his house, waiting for his owner to come down. He would be holding something in his mouth: a dishtowel from the kitchen, a ball, or sometimes his owner's cap or gloves. Being able to give something to his friend made Topper happy.

- Do you like giving things to other people?
- Can you remember a time when you gave something to someone?
- How did it make you feel?

A long time ago God gave His Son Jesus to the world. That made God happy because He loved all the people of the world and wanted to give them something wonderful. God sent Jesus to live on earth so people could get to know Jesus and love Him. God's love is a wonderful gift. Giving God's love to others makes us happy and makes other people happy too.

- How can you give God's love to other people this week?
- How can you give God *your* love?

▼ ▼ ▼

Bible Verse
God so loved the world that he gave his only Son. John 3:16 (NRSV)

For Older Children
Read and memorize the rest of John 3:16.

Let's Pray
Dear God, You have given me many gifts. Make me glad to give gifts to others, especially the gift of Your love.

Wasters and Savers

Are you a waster or a saver? Most people in our country waste a lot of things they could save. They crumple up and throw away paper they could use. They let the water faucet run when they're not using it. They let lights burn when they don't need them. They throw away food they could eat.

In poor countries people try hard to save what they have. The children there are taught to take care of their clothes and not lose them. Billy lost six of his jackets one winter. What do you think his mother said to him about that?

In our country some people save old newspapers, bottles, and cans. That's called *recycling*. The papers and magazines are used to make more paper. The bottles and cans are melted and used to make new bottles and cans.

- What do you think God wants you to be—a waster or a saver?
- Do you know why God wants us all to save and not waste what He gives us?

One reason we should save things instead of wasting them is so we'll have more to give to people who need help. Are you helping to feed any poor people? There are many hungry people in other countries as well as in our own. How can you help some of them?

- What are some things you waste?
- What can you start saving this week?

▼ ▼ ▼

Bible Verse
Let us . . . find [the ability] to help in time of need. Hebrews 4:16 (NRSV)

For Older Children
In Luke 15:11-24 Jesus told a story about a young man who wasted everything his father had given him. Note what his father did when he was sorry and came back home.

Let's Pray
Lord God, make me be a saver instead of a waster so I'll be able to help people who need help.

Brothers and Sisters

Sometimes brothers and sisters don't get along very well. They say they don't like each other and quarrel and fight. But God wants us to love our brothers and sisters and be nice to them.

- Do you have a sister or brother?
- How do you treat each other?

In the Bible there's a story of twelve brothers. The second-youngest brother's name was Joseph. He was his father's favorite. His father gave him a special coat made of many colors.

- Do you know why Joseph's brothers hated him?

- What did they do to him?
- What did God do for Joseph?
- What did Joseph do for his brothers? Why?

Some brothers and sisters are best friends. They like to be with each other. They play with each other and share what they have with each other. They obey one of the main rules God has given to all people: Do for others what you want them to do for you. That's called the Golden Rule.

Jesus said "Whoever does what my Father in heaven wants him to do is my brother, my sister, or my mother." At another time He said, "My brothers [and sisters] are those who listen to the word of God and do it (Matthew 7:12)."

- How can you be a sister or brother to Jesus?
- How will sisters and brothers of Jesus get along when they love each other the way Jesus loves them?

▼ ▼ ▼

Bible Verse
Jesus said, "Whoever does what my Father in heaven wants him to do is my brother, my sister, and my mother." Matthew 12:50 (TEV)

For Older Children
You can read more about Joseph and his brothers in Genesis 37:1-11.

Let's Pray
Dear Jesus, please keep me as a brother or sister by helping me do what God wants me to do.

Christians Who Run Out of Gas

People who own cars sometimes run out of gas. When the car runs out of gas, the engine dies, and the car can't go anywhere.

Some toys need batteries to run. When the batteries wear out, the toys don't work anymore.

Furnaces that burn oil need oil to work. When an oil furnace has used up the oil in its tank, it stops burning. If the furnace stops burning, it can't make any heat, and then the house gets cold.

- What's the only way to get a car started if it runs out of gas?
- How do you make toys work again when their batteries die?
- And what's the only way to get an oil furnace started if it has no oil in its tank?

A Christian's life is like a car that needs gas, a toy that needs batteries, or a furnace that needs oil. Do you know what the gas is that keeps our faith in Jesus burning and makes our hearts warm with God's love? It's the Holy Spirit. We get the Holy Spirit from God when we believe in Jesus and love Him.

Do you know how you can keep your heart filled with the Holy Spirit? By hearing and reading and learning about our heavenly Father and His Son Jesus. When we have God's Holy Spirit, then the furnace that burns in our hearts keeps us warm and happy. So we need to ask God to keep our hearts filled with the Holy Spirit.

▼ ▼ ▼

Bible Verse
God . . . gives you his Holy Spirit. 1 Thessalonians 4:8 (TEV)

For Older Children
You can read about the Holy Spirit in John 14:15-17.

Let's Pray
Dear God, please keep my heart filled with Your Holy Spirit. Help me to read and hear and learn more about You and Jesus.

Getting Even with Others

While running in the playground one day, Keith accidentally ran into Kevin and knocked him down. "I'll get even with you!" Kevin shouted angrily.

- What did Kevin mean when he said, "I'll get even with you"?
- What do children usually do to get even?

In Sunday school Keith learned the Golden Rule. Jesus mentioned it in several ways. He said, "Whatever you want others to do for you, do that for them." At another time he said, "Love your neighbor as yourself."

Keith decided to get even with people who did *good* things for him. When his mother made his favorite breakfast, Keith got even by doing the dishes without being asked. When his teacher was nice to him, Keith got even by telling her what a good teacher she was.

- How did getting even with others for *good* things they did change Keith's life?
- What do you suppose were some of the things he began to do?

When you're with other people, think about how you want them to treat you, and then do those things for others.

- What are some things you wish others would do for you?
- What happens when people treat others the way they'd like to be treated?
- If you were your parents, what would you like your children to do for you?

As you go to school and play with your friends this week, think of ways you can get even with them by doing good.

▼ ▼ ▼

Bible Verse
You must love your neighbor as yourself. Mark 12:31 (HBC)

For Older Children
Make a list of *good* things you will do for others this week.

Let's Pray
Dear Father in heaven, please help me to treat others the way I want to be treated.

Heroes in the Bible

Did you know that the Bible has a hall of fame? Every person mentioned in it was a hero. A hero is usually someone who has done something great.

In the Bible there are Noah and Abraham and Sarah and Joseph and Moses and King David and many more.

- Do you know about any Bible heroes?

■ What did they do?

The heroes in the Bible all believed God and obeyed Him even when it was difficult. Noah built an ark and believed God would take care of him and his family. Abraham and Sarah moved to a faraway country. They believed God wanted them to do that. Joseph was kidnapped by his brothers, but wasn't afraid. He believed God would have it all turn out good, and it did.

Have you ever thought of Jesus as the greatest hero in the Bible? What did Jesus do? Why do so many people love and worship Him?

Jesus promised to help you be a hero for Him. He said to His disciples, "I have set you an example, that you also should do as I have done."

■ What does Jesus want you to be?
■ What does He want you to do?

▼ ▼ ▼

Bible Verse
Christ . . . left you an example. He [did] no sin. 1 Peter 2:21-22 (TEV)

For Older Children
You can read about Abraham and Sarah in Hebrews 11:8-12.

Let's Pray
Lord Jesus, you are my best hero. Make me your kind of hero.

The Most Important Church Members

A man asked some children how they would pick up a dollar bill if they found one. What do you think they answered? Why didn't they say, "With my toes" or "With my nose"?

God has given our bodies many different parts. The Bible says each part does something special for the body.

- What do eyes do?
- What do feet do?
- What do hands do?
- What do ears do?

Our ears can't do what our eyes do and our eyes can't do what our ears do. Each part of our body is important.

The Bible says the church is like a body. It has many different parts, and all of them are special. No one part is like any other. That means that in Jesus' church every person is important.

There are several reasons why you are important to Jesus. Besides loving you, He has some things He wants you to do for Him.

- What are some things Jesus wants you to do now?
- What do you think you might do for Him when you're older?

Jesus loved children very much. Once He said children were the most important people in His church. He wanted older people to be like children.

- Why do you think Jesus loved children so much?
- How do you think people should be like children?

▼ ▼ ▼

Bible Verse
Jesus said, "Unless you change and become like children, you will never get into the kingdom of heaven." Matthew 18:3 (HBC)

For Older Children
In Mark 10:13-16 you can read how Jesus treated some children one day.

Let's Pray
Lord Jesus, I'm glad You think I'm very important. Help me to love and obey You.

Friends

Everybody wants to have friends. Friends are special people.

- What makes people friends?
- Who are some of your friends?
- What do you like most about your friends?

The Bible says, "A friend loves at all times." The Bible also says, "A friend sticks closer than a brother [or sister]."

- What does it mean to "love at all times"?
- How does your good friend stick by you?

Long ago there was a man whose name was Abraham. He was called a friend of God. Abraham obeyed God and talked to God.

- Why did God call Abraham His friend?
- Would you like to be called God's friend?

There's a song that says, "My best friend is Jesus." Even though you can't see or touch Jesus, He can be your best friend.

He is always with you and will always listen to you and love you. You can tell Jesus anything and He'll understand and help you.

Jesus wants to be friends with you. He said, "You are my friends if you do what I tell you to do (John 8:31)."

- How can you know what Jesus wants you to do?
- How can you show that you are a friend of Jesus?

▼ ▼ ▼

Bible Verse
A friend loves at all times. Proverbs 17:17 (NRSV)

For Older Children
Make a list of your friends. Don't forget to include your best friend Jesus. Then thank God for giving you your friends, especially Jesus.

Let's Pray
Dear Jesus, please continue to be my friend. Show me what You want me to do.

Liars and Lies

"It's a lie!" Buddy yelled at his friend, Brian. "You're a liar!" Brian yelled back at Buddy.

- What's a lie?
- Who is a liar?

Telling a lie is saying something that's not true. So why do a lot of people tell lies? What kinds of feelings do people get when they are caught telling lies?

Lies can hurt other people.

- Can you remember a lie someone told about another person?
- How did the lie hurt that person?
- When your parents say, "Tell me the truth," what do they mean?

Telling people the truth is another way of loving them. That's why the Bible says, "Do not lie to one another."

Jesus always said what was true. He scolded people when they lied.

- What would happen if we always lied whenever we said anything?
- What can you do to get rid of lies?

The next time you're tempted to tell a lie, ask God to help you tell the truth instead.

▼ ▼ ▼

Bible Verse
Do not lie to one another. Colossians 3:9 (TEV)

For Older Children
Write a little story about a child who told a lie. Tell how the child got rid of the lie.

Let's Pray
Dear Jesus, I'm sorry I don't always tell the truth. Please forgive me. I don't want to be a liar.

When Children Help

Can you imagine how big a room it would take to hold five million children? That's a lot of kids! On a television program five million children called and promised to help others in some way. All together they promised to do 31 million hours of free work. That's more than six hours of work for each child who called.

- What do you think were some of the things the children promised to do?

They promised to scrub graffiti off walls and sidewalks. They said they would wash windows at home. They promised to sweep streets and clean beaches. Some said they would pick up cans and bottles and other trash along their roads.

- What are some things you could do to make life better for others?
- How about cutting the lawn or shoveling snow for a neighbor?
- How about going to a store for a person who lives alone and doesn't have a car?

The Bible says we should carry each other's burdens. Do you know what that means? It means that we should help each other. Burdens are troubles or problems or work. So "Carry each other's burdens" means "Help others do what they have to do or help them with their problems."

Jesus suffered for us so we could have forgiveness and life with God. He carries our burdens and helps us when we're sad or need help. When we're thankful to Him for that, we're glad to do things for others. Try it. You'll see.

▼ ▼ ▼

Bible Verse
Help each other with your problems. Galatians 6:2 (HBC)

For Older Children
Tomorrow ask two people what you can do for them.

Let's Pray
Lord Jesus, You help me in so many ways. Make me willing to help others.

One of God's Helpers

Not long ago there was a man whose name was Albert Schweitzer. He was a writer, a doctor, and a very good organ player. When Albert was a young man, he decided to study whatever he wanted until he was thirty years old. But he promised God that when he became thirty years old, he would start to help other people.

At first Albert studied about Jesus and the Bible and how to play the piano and the organ. On his thirtieth birthday he remembered his promise to do things for others. So he began helping prisoners who were let out of jail. He also helped children without parents.

One day young Albert read about how much people in Africa needed doctors. So for the next seven years he studied to become a doctor, and then he went to Africa. There he started a hospital and worked very hard to make sick people well. He lived until he was ninety years old and helped lots of people while he was alive.

Dr. Schweitzer said helping others was a duty, something he

ought to do. He said he did his work because of what Jesus had done for him. By helping others he became a worker for God.

Jesus once told a story about a man who helped someone who needed help. That helper is called the Good Samaritan. When he was on a trip he saw someone lying by the side of the road. The man had been beaten by robbers and needed a doctor. No one else had stopped to help, but the Good Samaritan stopped and took the man to a place where he could get help.

You don't have to wait until you're grown up to be one of God's helpers. You can start to help others right now.

- How can you help your parents?
- How can you help some older people living near you?

▼ ▼ ▼

Bible Verse
Do for others just what you want them to do for you. Luke 6:31 (TEV)

For Older Children
You can read about the Good Samaritan in Luke 10:25-37.

Let's Pray
Lord Jesus, You have given me a good rule to follow. Help me to do it.

Paintings and Painters

Have you ever been to an art museum? There are many art museums in the world. Almost every city has one.

- Why do people go to art museums?
- What kinds of paintings do you like to look at?

■ What kind of pictures would you paint if you were a painter?

Good painters try to show us something they see and feel. What a painter sees is often very different from what we see. That's one reason many paintings are interesting. Paintings show us how different people see different things.

Paintings can teach people. They can tell us what God has done and what He's still doing. Trees, flowers, mountains, animals, the ocean, and fish in the lakes and rivers—what do you think they tell us about God?

Painters also can tell what God has done for people and what He still does. Many of the paintings in museums show what the Bible tells about God. Lots of paintings tell about Jesus and how He died for us.

- What story from Jesus' life would you like to paint?
- What else would you like to paint?

The Bible says we should tell others about the wonderful things God has done. How can paintings do that?

▼ ▼ ▼

Bible Verse
You are . . . God's own people, chosen to proclaim the wonderful acts of God. 1 Peter 2:9 (TEV)

For Older Children
Make a list of ways you can communicate (say things) to others. Circle what you'd like to be good at, like writing, singing, or painting.

Let's Pray
Lord, my God, make me someone who can tell others—maybe even through pictures—what You have done for them, especially what You have done for everyone through Your Son Jesus.

Having a Good Laugh

There are different kinds of laughter. There are giggling and guffawing. There are little laughs and great big belly laughs.

- What makes you laugh?
- How do you feel when you laugh?
- When do you laugh the most?

Doctors who try to help people feel good say that laughing is like a medicine. It makes people feel better. They even have people practice laughing together.

- How does laughing with someone make you feel?

In countries like China there are many people called Buddhists. They learn the teachings of a man called Buddha. Sometimes he is shown laughing.

- Do you think Jesus ever laughed?
- What are some things you think Jesus may have laughed about?

It's good to laugh, but it's never good to laugh at someone.

- What does it mean to laugh at someone?
- Why do children sometimes laugh at other children?
- How do you feel when someone laughs at you?

It's good to laugh *with* others, but wrong to laugh *at* anyone. Have lots of good laughs this week, but don't laugh at anyone — except maybe yourself.

▼ ▼ ▼

Bible Verse
[God] will yet fill your mouth with laughter, and your lips with shouts of joy. Job 8:21 (NRSV)

For Older Children
Ecclesiastes 3:1-8 says there is a right time for everything. What does it say in verse 4?

Let's Pray
Dear God, I'm glad that laughter is good for me. Please fill my life with laughter, but help me to know the right and wrong times to laugh.

INDEX

Index of Bible Passages

Text	Theme	Page
Genesis 1:11	What We All Can't Do	105
Exodus 20:3	Let's Talk About God	110
Exodus 20:7	Bad Words and Good Words	47
Exodus 20:12	Does Your Mother Work?	29
1 Samuel 16:7	A Good Heart	64
2 Samuel 6:5	When People Play	144
Job 8:21	Having a Good Laugh	163
Psalm 24:1	What Do You Own?	59
Psalm 34:7	Avoiding Dangers	41
Psalm 38:18	Are You Ever Ashamed?	25
Psalm 91:4	What Scares You?	28
Psalm 91:11	What About Angels?	115
Psalm 92:1	How to Say "Thanks"	85
Psalm 100:2	Children Singing	142
Psalm 119:105	When It's Dark Outside	92
Psalm 122:1	Going to Church	93
Psalm 139:14	Whatever God Has Made	73
Psalm 143:10	Deciding Which Way to Go	56
Psalm 145:9	Loving Children Who Are Different	137
Psalm 146:7	The Gifts of Food and Water	77
Psalm 148:12-13	Talking to Grandma and Grandpa	133
Psalm 150:6	Making Music	103
Proverbs 6:6	It's Fun to Work	63
Proverbs 10:23	Being a Good Sport	65
Proverbs 11:13	Keeping a Secret	131
Proverbs 12:2	Cruel Children	134
Proverbs 12:10	Taking Care of Your Pet	58
Proverbs 17:17	Friends	155
Ecclesiastes 3:11	Knowing the Right Time	16
Ecclesiastes 3:17	Things You're Ready to Do	53
Ecclesiastes 12:1	What If You Couldn't Remember Anything?	13

Isaiah 1:18	When It Snows	71
Isaiah 9:6	Wonders in the World	76
Isaiah 40:31	Why Be Sad?	109
Daniel 1:8	What Do You Eat?	126
Matthew 2:1-2	You Can Be a Star	97
Matthew 5:9	You Can Be a Peacemaker	38
Matthew 5:16	How Bright a Light Are You?	36
Matthew 12:50	Brothers and Sisters	148
	A Happy Home	52
Matthew 13:45	Choosing the Best	89
Matthew 18:3	The Most Important Church Members	154
Matthew 28:19	Going to Faraway Places	80
Matthew 28:20	How Brave Are You?	48
	Your Teachers	129
Mark 12:31	Getting Even with Others	151
Luke 2:11	What Do You Like About Christmas?	120
Luke 2:46	Your Sunday School	111
Luke 6:31	One of God's Helpers	160
Luke 8:8	If You Couldn't Hear	60
Luke 12:24	Bird Nests and Little Birds	79
John 3:16	Love Is . . .	96
	The Fun of Giving	145
John 10:27	Being a Christian	98
John 14:9	Knowing Jesus	100
John 15:5	Grape Vines and Branches	106
John 20:31	Good Reasons for Reading	50
Acts 10:34	What's Fair?	87
Acts 14:17	When It Rains	82
Acts 20:35	Why Giving Is Better Than Receiving	128
2 Corinthians 1:20	Remembering What You Promised	20
2 Corinthians 5:15	Learning From Geese	75
2 Corinthians 9:7	Getting an Allowance	55
Galatians 3:26	What's Your Name?	14
Galatians 6:2	When Children Help	159
Galatians 5:1	What About Rules?	88
Ephesians 1:7	Will You Forgive Me?	37

Ephesians 4:15	Who Are Your Heroes?	66
Ephesians 4:25	Is Honesty the Best Policy?	140
Ephesians 4:32	Are You a Bossy Person?	12
Ephesians 5:20	The Man Who Said "Thank You"	139
Ephesians 5:16	The Best Use of Your Time	23
Ephesians 6:1	You and Your Parents	44
Philippians 2:9	Names of God	113
Philippians 2:14	Learning Not to Grumble	46
Philippians 4:11	Wishing	34
Philippians 4:6	Let's See Your Teeth	68
Colossians 3:9	Liars and Lies	156
Colossians 3:23	What Do You Want to Be?	18
1 Thessalonians 4:8	Christians Who Run Out of Gas	149
1 Thess. 5:16-18	Why Pray?	104
1 Timothy 6:18	The Best Way to Be Rich	42
Hebrews 4:16	Wasters and Savers	147
James 1:17	Your Bag of Gifts	22
James 1:19	People Who Get Angry	138
1 Peter 2:9	Paintings and Painters	162
1 Peter 3:22	Where Is Heaven?	114
1 Peter 2:21-22	Heroes in the Bible	152
1 Peter 5:7	Your Worries and Fears	32
2 Peter 3:18	Why Go To School?	43
1 John 1:9	Why Not Admit It?	31
Revelation 1:18	Easter Eggs and Rabbits	121
Revelation 3:3	How Good Are Your Manners?	24
Revelation 17:14	If You Were King or Queen	91

Topical Index of Contents

You may want to converse with a child on particular occasions or for specific needs and purposes. Listed are concerns and aspects of Christian life and growth that the conversations in the book will help you address.

Topic	Theme	Page
Admitting sins	Remembering What You Promised	18
	Why Not Admit It?	30
Angels	Avoiding Dangers	39
	What About Angels?	115
Anger	People Who Get Angry	137
Bad words	Bad Words and Good Words	46
Being afraid	How Brave Are You?	47
	What Scares You?	26
	Your Worries and Fears	31
Being ashamed	Are You Ever Ashamed?	24
Being bossy	Are You a Bossy Person?	11
Being brave	How Brave Are You?	47
Being a Christian	Being a Christian	97
Being cruel	Cruel Children	134
	Having a Good Laugh	162
Being helpful	A Happy Home	51
Being like Jesus	Wishing	33
The Bible	When It's Dark Outside	91
Brothers and sisters	Brothers and Sisters	142
	A Happy Home	51
Cheating	Being a Good Sport	64
Children	The Most Important Church Members	153
Choices	Choosing the Best	88
	Deciding Which Way to Go	55
Christmas	The Fun of Giving	145
	What Do You Like About Christmas?	119
	How You Can Be a Star	96
Church	Going to Church	93
	The Most Important Church Members	153

	Your Sunday School	110
Complaining	Learning Not to Grumble	45
Creation	What We All Can't Do	104
	Whatever God Has Made	72
Danger	Avoiding Dangers	39
Darkness	When It's Dark Outside	91
Deciding what to do	Deciding Which Way to Go	55
Doing things for others	Brothers and Sisters	142
	Grapevines and Branches	106
	What Do You Want to Be?	16
Easter	Easter Eggs and Rabbits	120
Eating good foods	What Do You Eat?	125
Fairness	What's Fair?	86
Food	The Gifts of Food and Water	77
	What Do You Eat?	125
Forgetting	What If You Couldn't Remember Anything?	12
Forgiveness	When It Snows	71
	Why Not Admit It?	30
	Will You Forgive Me?	36
Freedom	What About Rules?	87
Friends	Friends	154
Getting even	Getting Even with Others	150
Giving and receiving	The Fun of Giving	145
	Why Giving Is Better Than Receiving	126
God's care	Bird Nests and Little Birds	78
	The Gifts of Food and Water	77
	Let's See Your Teeth	67
	What About Angels?	115
	Why Be Sad?	108
	Your Worries and Fears	31
God's love	The Fun of Giving	145
	When It Snows	71
	Will You Forgive Me?	36
God's plan for you	What We All Can't Do	104
God's promises	Remembering What You Promised	18

	When It Rains	81
Good sportsman-ship	Being a Good Sport	64
Grandparents	Talking to Grandma and Grandpa	131
Growing up	What Do You Want to Be?	16
Grumbling	Learning Not to Grumble	45
Having a good heart	A Good Heart	63
Hearing	If You Couldn't Hear	59
Heaven	Where Is Heaven?	113
Helping others	How Bright a Light Are You?	34
	Learning From Geese	73
	The Best Way to Be Rich	41
	One of God's Helpers	159
	Wasters and Savers	146
	When Children Help	157
Heroes	Heroes in the Bible	151
	Who Are Your Heroes?	65
Holy Spirit	Christians Who Run Out of Gas	149
Home	Brothers and Sisters	142
	A Happy Home	51
Honesty	Is Honesty the Best Policy?	139
Honoring Jesus	What's Your Name?	13
Honoring your parents	Does Your Mother Work?	28
	You and Your Parents	44
Kindness	Are You a Bossy Person?	11
	Cruel Children	134
	Taking Care of Your Pet	56
Knowing Jesus	If You Were a King or Queen	90
	Knowing Jesus	100
Laughing	Having a Good Laugh	162
Laziness	It's Fun to Work	62
Learning	Good Reasons for Reading	50
	Why Go To School?	42
	Your Sunday School	110
Listening	Being a Christian	97
	If You Couldn't Hear	59

Love	Love Is . . .	95
Loving people who are different	Cruel Children	134
	Loving Children Who Are Different	136
Loving God	Let's Talk About God	109
Loving others	The Best Way to Be Rich	41
	Friends	154
	Liars and Lies	155
Lying	Is Honesty the Best Policy?	139
	Liars and Lies	155
Manners	How Good Are Your Manners?	23
Money	Getting an Allowance	54
	The Best Way to Be Rich	41
Music	Making Music	101
Names	Names of God	112
	What's Your Name?	13
Obedience	What About Rules?	87
	You and Your Parents	44
Owning things	What Do You Own?	58
Peace	You Can Be a Peacemaker	37
Pets	Taking Care of Your Pet	56
Playing	Being a Good Sport	64
	How Good Are Your Manners?	23
	When People Play	142
Praising God	Children Singing	141
	Making Music	101
	Whatever God Has Made	72
Praying and prayer	Why Pray?	103
Promises	Remembering What You Promised	18
Rainbows	When It Rains	81
Reading	Good Reasons for Reading	50
Remembering	Remembering What You Promised	18
	What If You Couldn't Remember Anything?	12
Rules	What About Rules?	87
Sadness	Why Be Sad?	108
Saying "Thank You"	How to Say "Thanks"	85
	The Gifts of Food and Water	77
	Let's See Your Teeth	67

	The Man Who Said "Thank You"	138
School	Why Go To School?	42
Secrets	Keeping a Secret	130
Sharing	Getting an Allowance	54
Singing to God	Children Singing	141
Stars	How You Can Be a Star	96
Swearing	Bad Words and Good Words	46
Talents	Your Bag of Gifts	21
Talking to others	Love Is . . .	95
	Talking to Grandma and Grandpa	131
Teachers	Your Teachers	128
Telling the truth	Is Honesty the Best Policy?	139
	Liars and Lies	155
Telling others about God	The Best Way to Be Rich	41
	Going to Faraway Places	79
	How Bright a Light Are You?	34
	Paintings and Painters	160
	How You Can Be a Star	96
	Your Teachers	128
Time	Knowing the Right Time	15
	The Best Use of Your Time	
	Things You're Ready to Do	52
Traveling	Going to Faraway Places	79
Wasting and saving	Wasters and Savers	146
Wishing	Wishing	33
Wonders of the world	Wonders in the World	75
Working	It's Fun to Work	62
Worrying	Your Worries and Fears	31

About the Author

DR. ALLAN JAHSMANN is a former teacher, pastor, psychologist, and editor of church school resources for children and adults. He is the author of many books for children, including the bestselling *Little Visits with God* and *More Little Visits with God.*

For many years, Dr. Jahsmann was the editor of *Interaction*, a monthly magazine for church school workers, and a magazine of daily readings for young Christians called *My Devotions.* Some of his other books include *Leading Children into the Bible, Power Beyond Words, How You Too Can Teach*, and *The Holy Bible for Children*, a simplified and abridged translation of the Bible.

In his eighties, Dr. Jahsmann still plays tennis regularly and is currently working on a book of conversations with the elderly. His main interest continues to be the Christian nurture of children.